The Party, After You Left

by Roz Chast

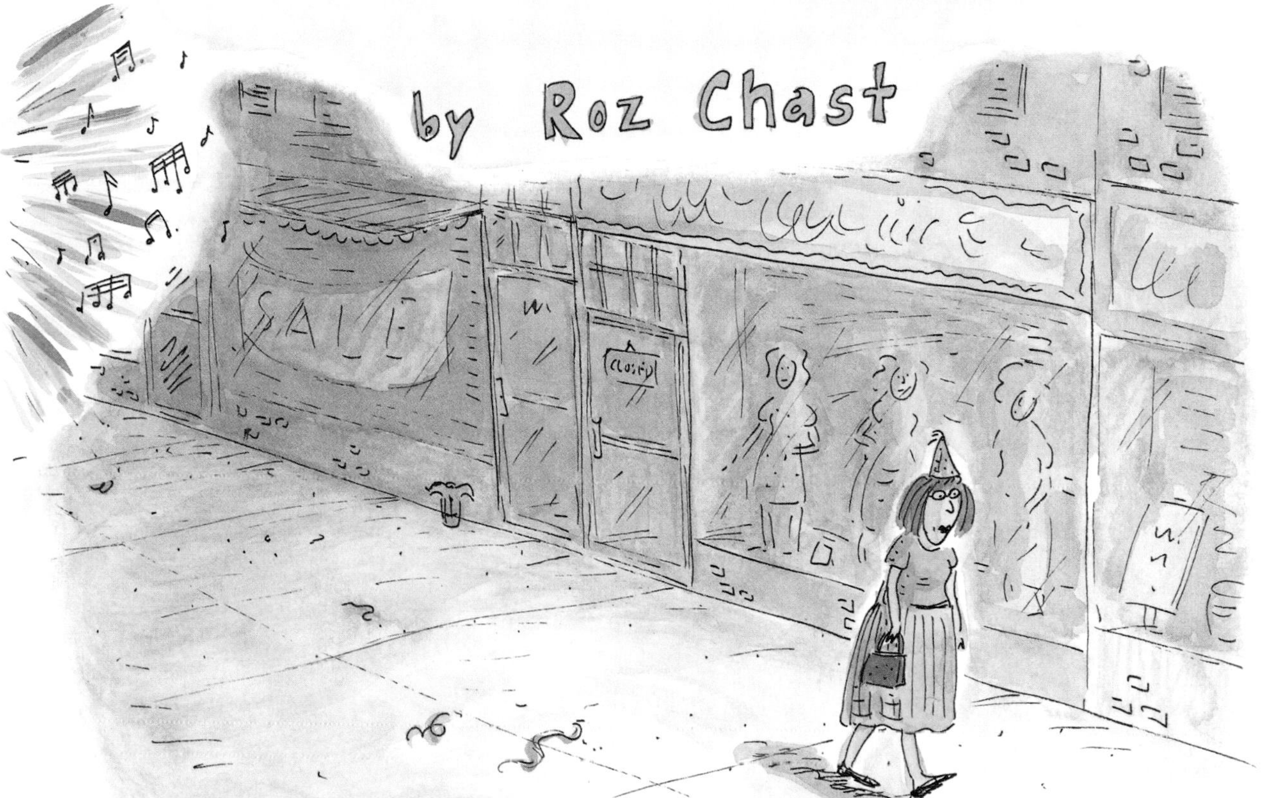
SALE
CLOSED

BLOOMSBURY

For information, address Bloomsbury, 175 Fifth Avenue, New York, New York 10010.

Published by Bloomsbury, New York and London.
Distributed to the trade by Holtzbrinck Publishers

All papers used by Bloomsbury are natural, recyclable products made from wood grown in sustainable, well-managed forests.

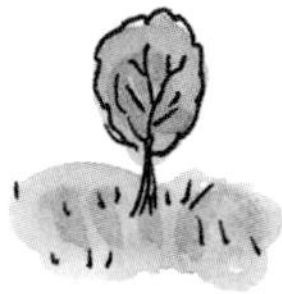

The manufacturing processes conform to the environmental regulations of the country of origin.

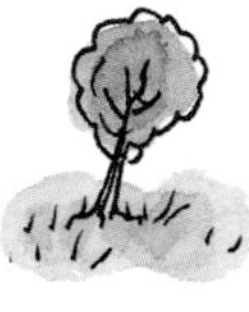

ISBN 1-58234-377-2

First U.S. Edition 2004

3 5 7 9 10 8 6 4 2

Printed and bound by C&C Offset Printing Co., Ltd., Hong Kong

GIFTS FROM THE
HOUSE OF LOW GOALS

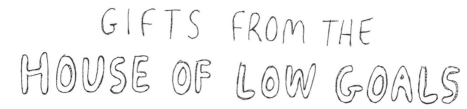

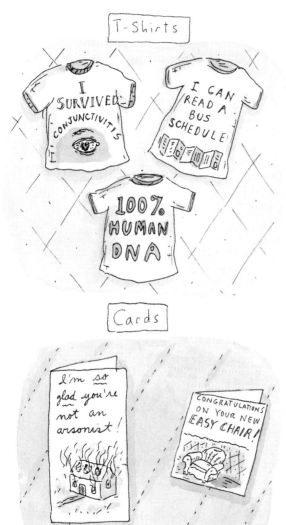

T-Shirts

I SURVIVED CONJUNCTIVITIS

I CAN READ A BUS SCHEDULE!

100% HUMAN DNA

Cards

I'm so glad you're not an arsonist!

CONGRATULATIONS ON YOUR NEW EASY CHAIR!

Special-Occasion Cakes

WOW! ONLY 6 CAVITIES!

HAPPY TATTOO REMOVAL!

NO LOITERING ARRESTS IN ONE YEAR!

Trophies

PARTICIPANT

R. Chr

THEORIES OF EVERYTHING

Everything's gone downhill since 1964.
Everything is my fault.
Everything IS your fault.
Everything would be perfect if I had a dirt bike.

AFGHANIGAP

Classic
Cargo
Pleated front
Flat front
Slim fit with Lycra
Relaxed fit
Cropped

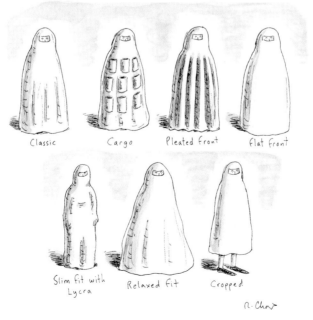

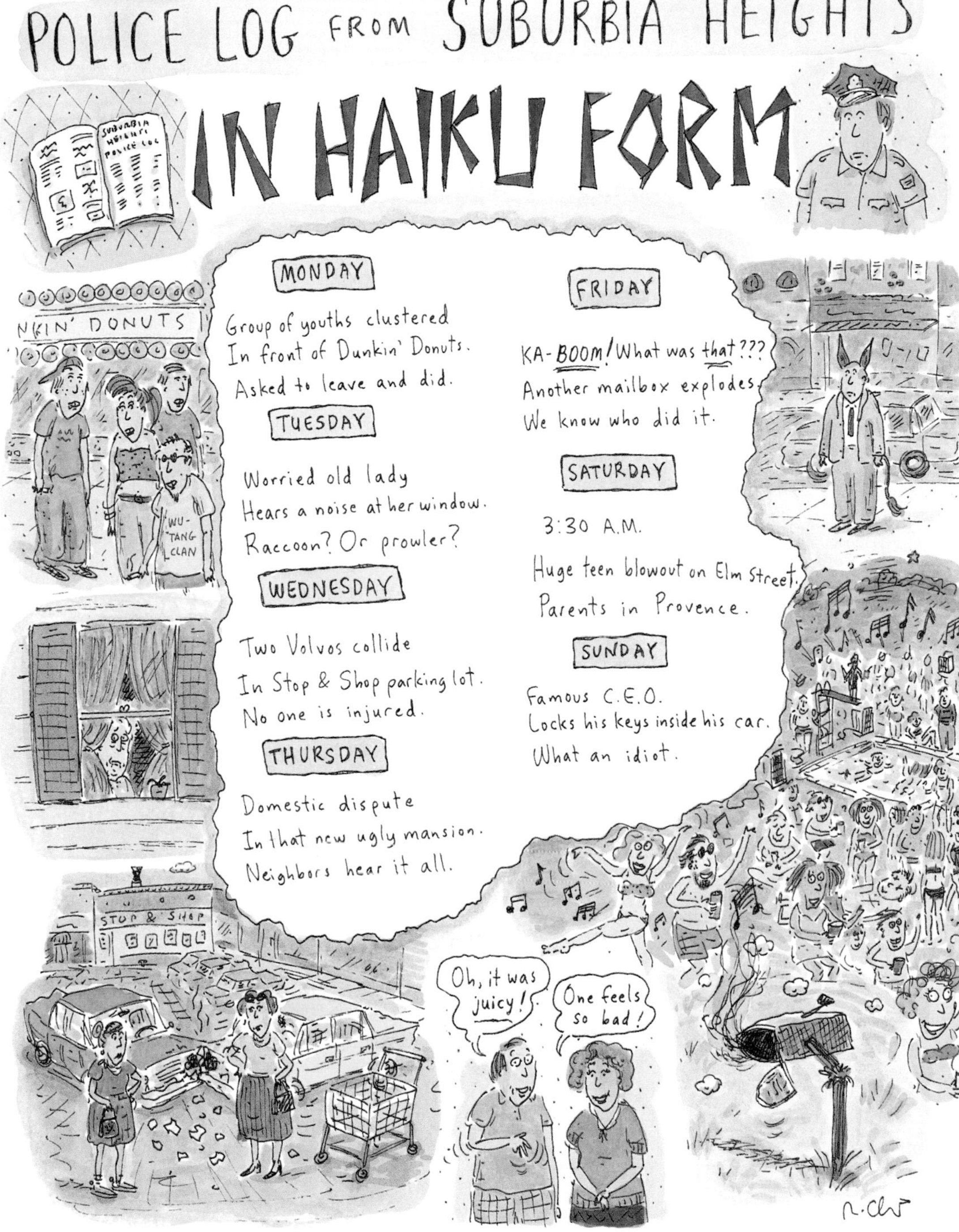
POLICE LOG FROM SUBURBIA HEIGHTS
IN HAIKU FORM
MONDAY
Group of youths clustered
In front of Dunkin' Donuts.
Asked to leave and did.
TUESDAY
Worried old lady
Hears a noise at her window.
Raccoon? Or prowler?
WEDNESDAY
Two Volvos collide
In Stop & Shop parking lot.
No one is injured.
THURSDAY
Domestic dispute
In that new ugly mansion.
Neighbors hear it all.
FRIDAY
KA-BOOM! What was that???
Another mailbox explodes.
We know who did it.
SATURDAY
3:30 A.M.
Huge teen blowout on Elm Street.
Parents in Provence.
SUNDAY
Famous C.E.O.
Locks his keys inside his car.
What an idiot.
WU-TANG CLAN
STOP & SHOP
Oh, it was juicy!
One feels so bad!

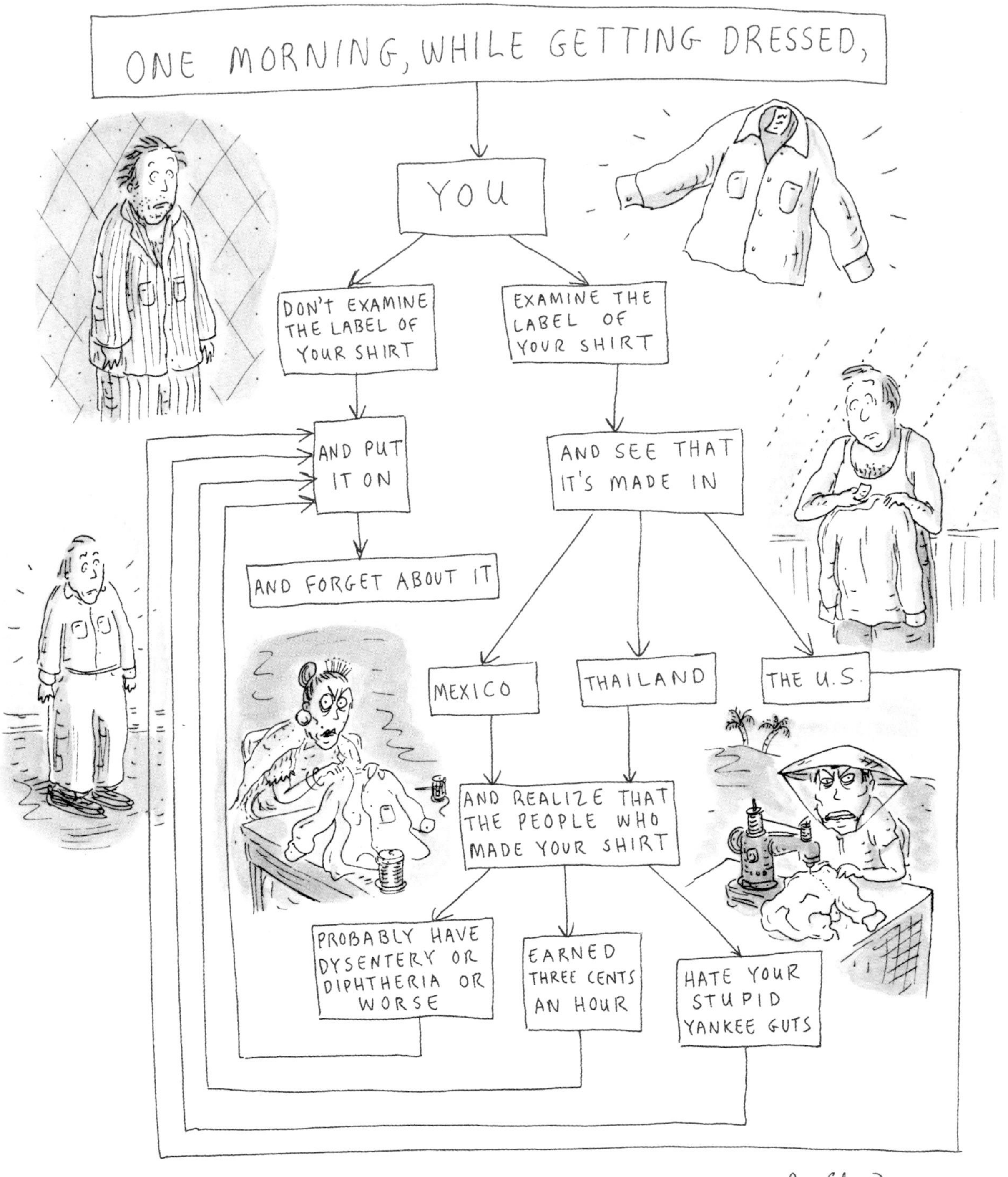
ONE MORNING, WHILE GETTING DRESSED,
YOU
DON'T EXAMINE THE LABEL OF YOUR SHIRT
EXAMINE THE LABEL OF YOUR SHIRT
AND PUT IT ON
AND FORGET ABOUT IT
AND SEE THAT IT'S MADE IN
MEXICO
THAILAND
THE U.S.
AND REALIZE THAT THE PEOPLE WHO MADE YOUR SHIRT
PROBABLY HAVE DYSENTERY OR DIPHTHERIA OR WORSE
EARNED THREE CENTS AN HOUR
HATE YOUR STUPID YANKEE GUTS
R. Chast

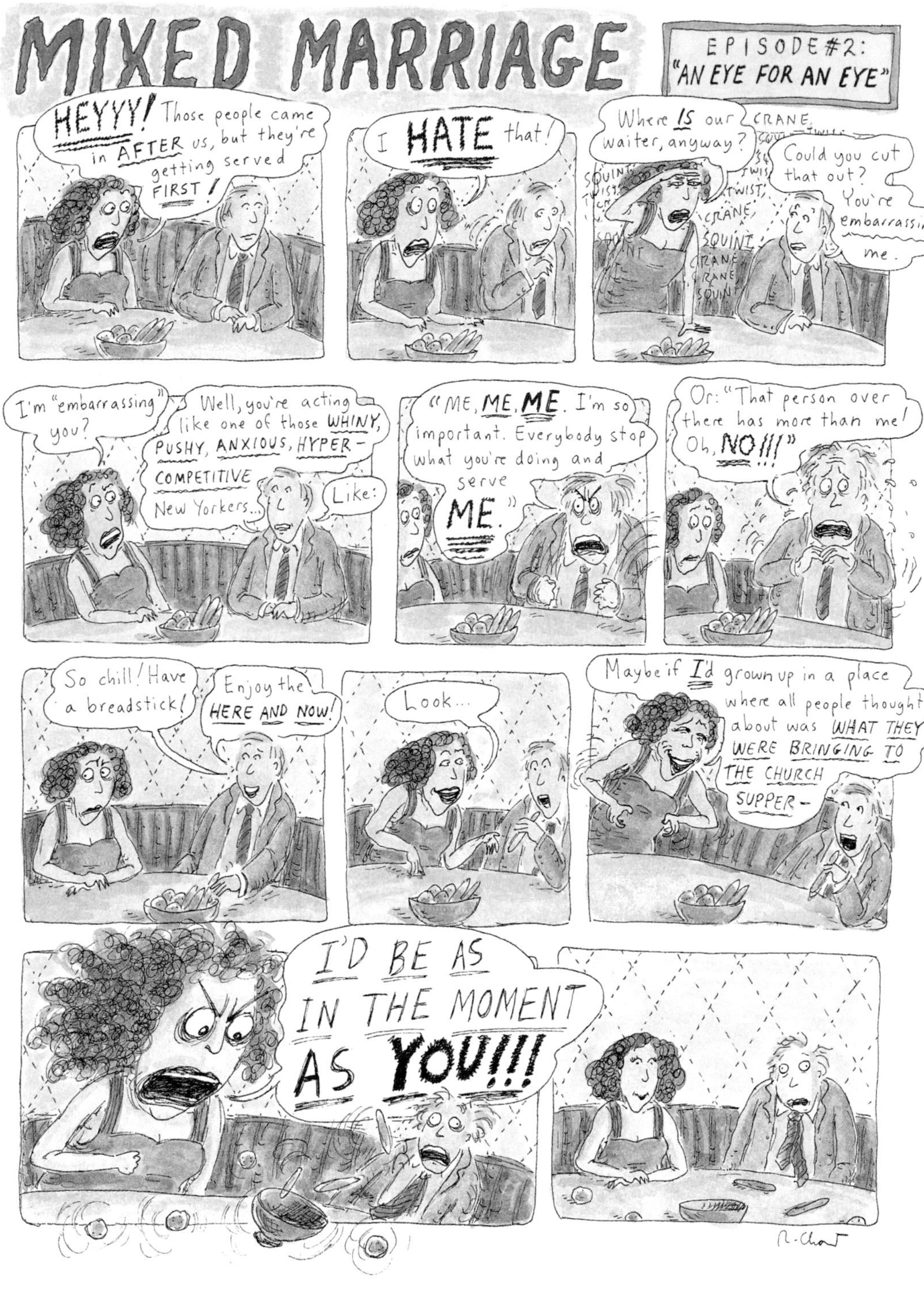
MIXED MARRIAGE
EPISODE #2: "AN EYE FOR AN EYE"
HEYYY! Those people came in AFTER us, but they're getting served FIRST!
I HATE that!
Where IS our waiter, anyway?
SQUINT TWIST CRANE TWIST CRANE SQUINT CRANE CRANE SQUINT
Could you cut that out? You're embarrassing me.
I'm "embarrassing" you?
Well, you're acting like one of those WHINY, PUSHY, ANXIOUS, HYPER-COMPETITIVE New Yorkers...
Like:
"ME, ME, ME. I'm so important. Everybody stop what you're doing and serve ME."
Or: "That person over there has more than me! Oh, NO!!!"
So chill! Have a breadstick!
Enjoy the HERE AND NOW!
Look...
Maybe if I'd grown up in a place where all people thought about was WHAT THEY WERE BRINGING TO THE CHURCH SUPPER-
I'D BE AS IN THE MOMENT AS YOU!!!

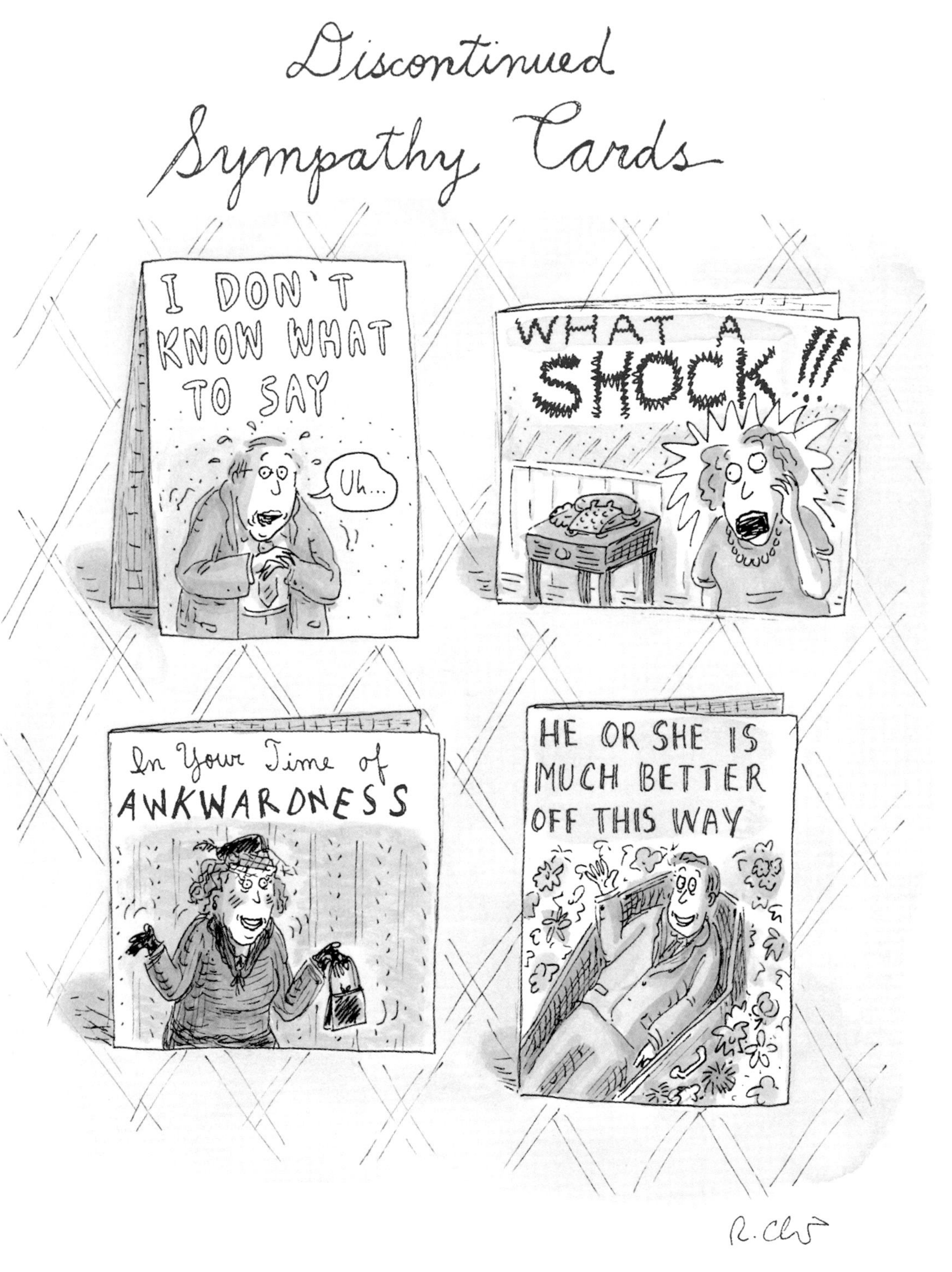
Discontinued Sympathy Cards
I DON'T KNOW WHAT TO SAY
Uh...
WHAT A SHOCK!!!
In Your Time of AWKWARDNESS
HE OR SHE IS MUCH BETTER OFF THIS WAY

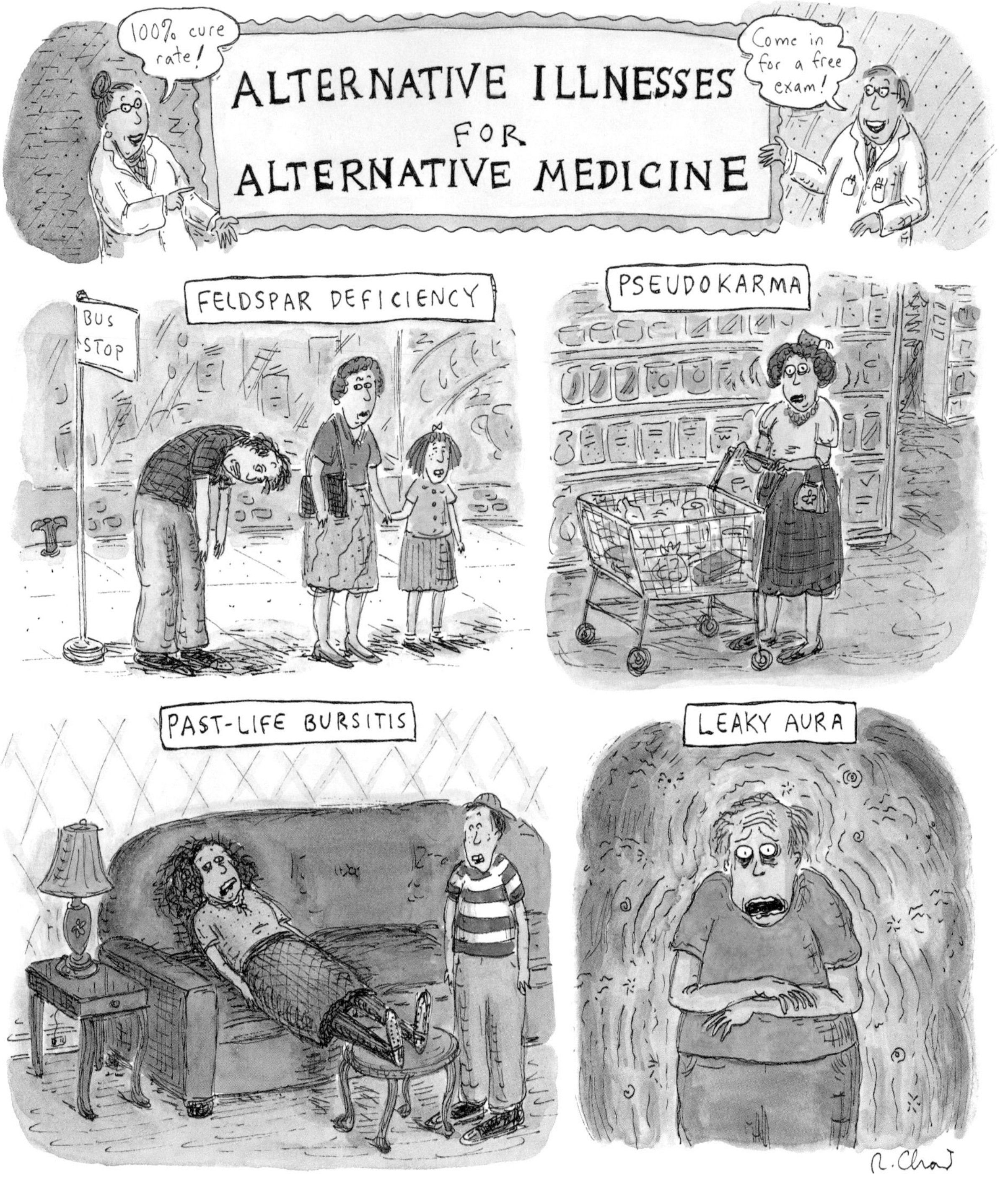
100% cure rate!
ALTERNATIVE ILLNESSES FOR ALTERNATIVE MEDICINE
Come in for a free exam!
FELDSPAR DEFICIENCY
BUS STOP
PSEUDOKARMA
PAST-LIFE BURSITIS
LEAKY AURA
R. Chast

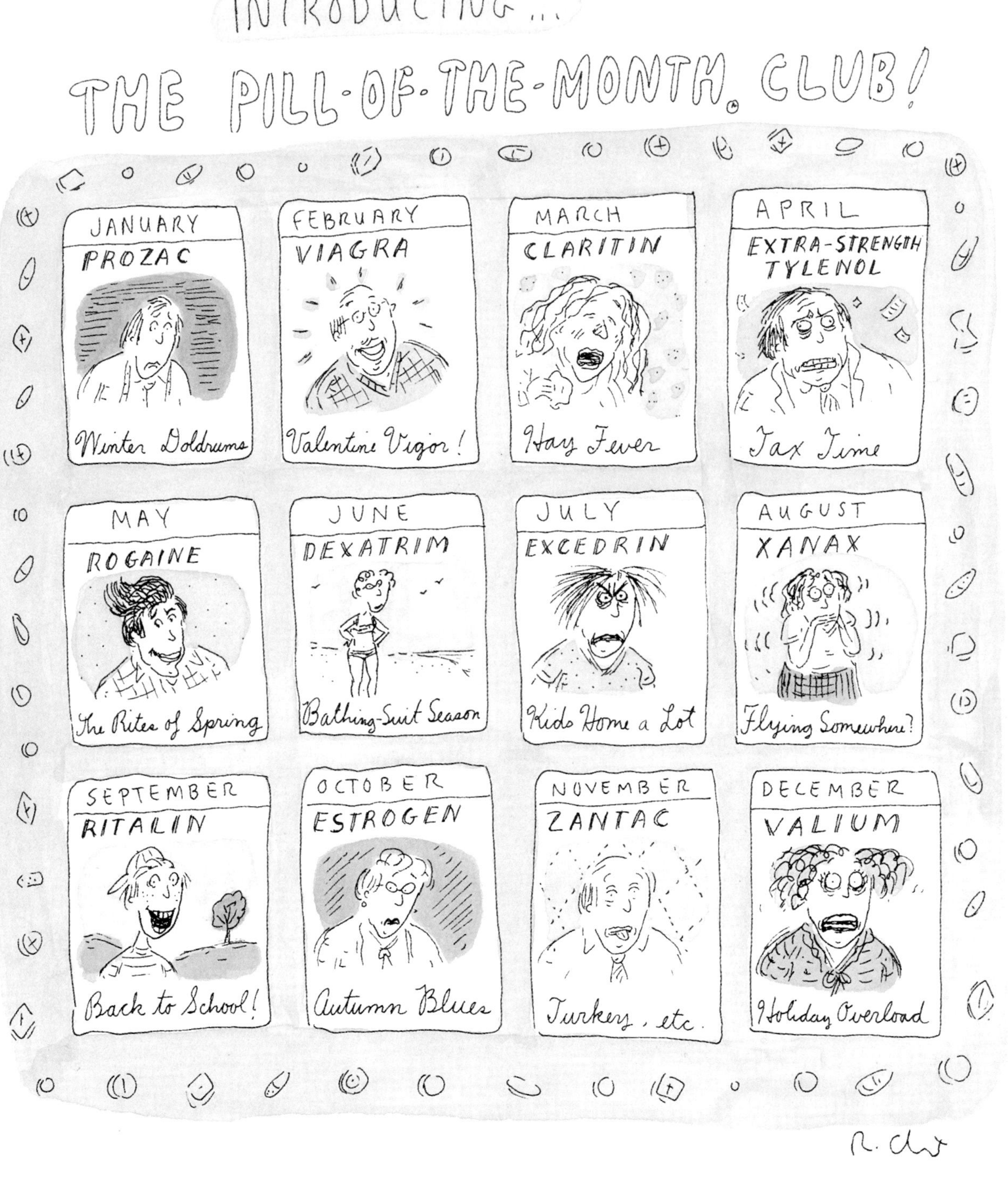
INTRODUCING...
THE PILL-OF-THE-MONTH CLUB!
JANUARY
PROZAC
Winter Doldrums
FEBRUARY
VIAGRA
Valentine Vigor!
MARCH
CLARITIN
Hay Fever
APRIL
EXTRA-STRENGTH TYLENOL
Tax Time
MAY
ROGAINE
The Rites of Spring
JUNE
DEXATRIM
Bathing-Suit Season
JULY
EXCEDRIN
Kids Home a Lot
AUGUST
XANAX
Flying Somewhere?
SEPTEMBER
RITALIN
Back to School!
OCTOBER
ESTROGEN
Autumn Blues
NOVEMBER
ZANTAC
Turkey, etc.
DECEMBER
VALIUM
Holiday Overload
R. Chast

ITEM #3715 - COZY CARDIGAN

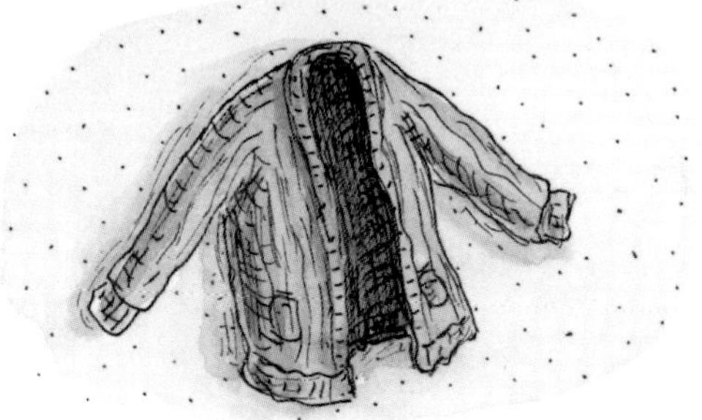

Snuggle up in this oh-so-cozy cardigan. Once you slip it on, you'll never want to take it off. We've improved the fit and the texture - it's a hug made of wool, a hug that never lets go before you're ready to be let go. Whether you're just sitting at home with your family, who must think you're some kind of automaton and take you for granted day in and day out, who can't be bothered to clean up after themselves, it's a wonder you're not a complete alcoholic, or whether you're going to work at the widget office where all day long, you have the privilege of watching your boss making goo-goo eyes at that thing in the black leather miniskirt that a normal person with her legs would never wear, and finally it's five o'clock and you can go home to your empty apartment overlooking two gas stations and a restaurant that is probably a Mafia money-laundering operation because it has all this expensive but ugly junk in it and about seven waiters per customer because no one ever eats there, and you wonder: is this all there is?, this is the sweater you'll reach for over and over again. We guarantee it!

Black, white, red, green, navy........S, M, L, XL - $39.95

R. Chast

THE BREAKUP

We'll always like you - as a friend!
The fact is you're too good for us! We don't DESERVE you!
Oh my God!! You've met somebody MORE QUALIFIED!!!
R. Chast

THE INSANITY PLEA
FOR PARKING OFFENSES
Heard the siren song of the hydrant.
I'm LONELY... so LONELY...
Thought "No Parking Anytime" did not apply to demigods.
NO PARKING ANYTIME
Was convinced that he and parking meter had a telepathic understanding.
You BETRAYED me!
R. Chast

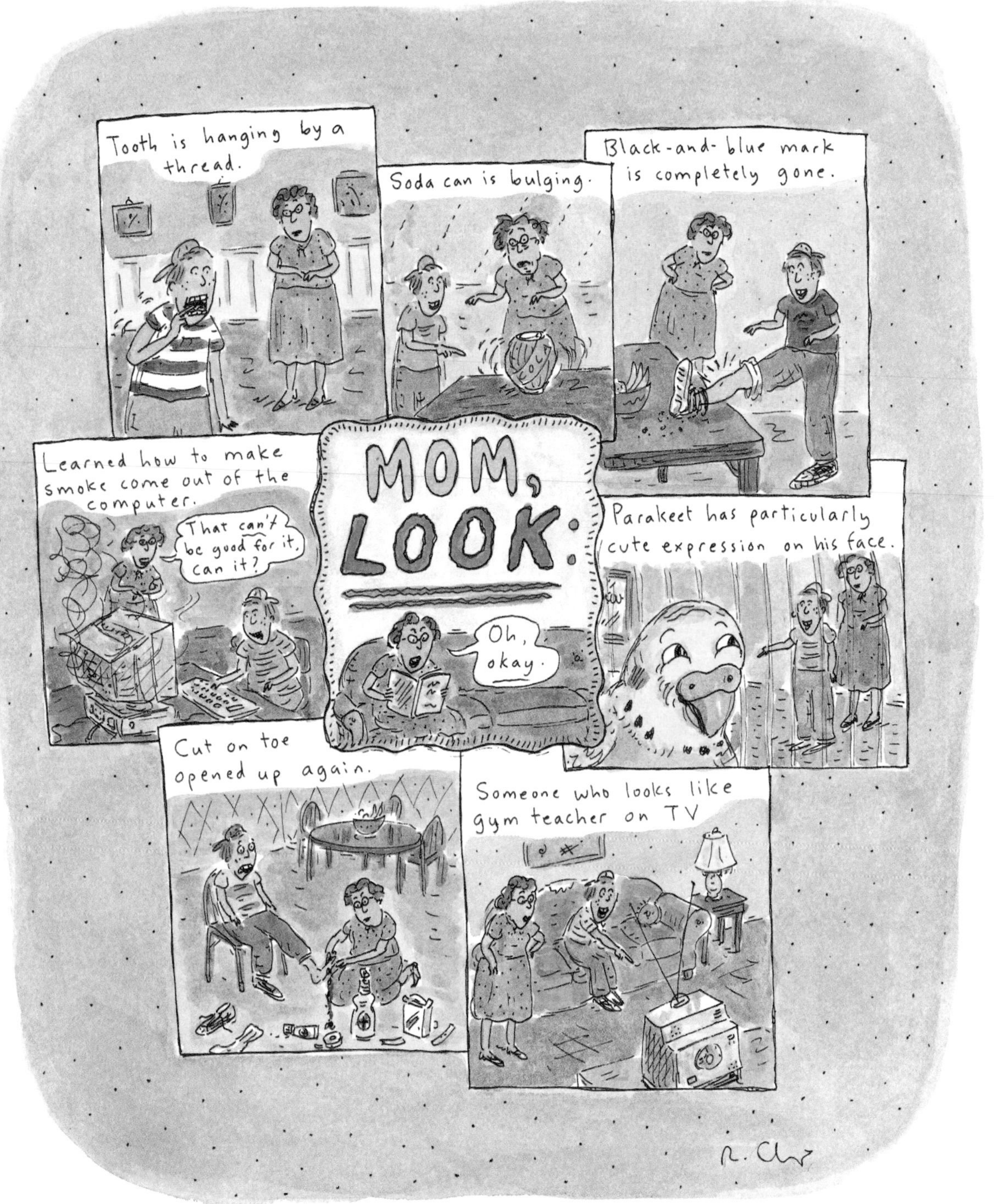
MOM, LOOK:
Oh, okay.
Tooth is hanging by a thread.
Soda can is bulging.
Black-and-blue mark is completely gone.
Learned how to make smoke come out of the computer.
That can't be good for it, can it?
Parakeet has particularly cute expression on his face.
Cut on toe opened up again.
Someone who looks like gym teacher on TV

INTRODUCING...
THE 1040-F.I.* FORM
* THE TAX RETURN FOR THE FINANCIALLY INCOMPETENT
① How much money do you guess you made last year?
Under $10,000.
Somewhere between $10,000 and $100,000.
More than $100,000, but I don't know how or why.
② Did you save any receipts?
I tried, but I just couldn't.
I think there're some in a shoebox. I'll go look.
No. What am I, an accountant?
③ Check payment preference.
How could I owe anything? My year was lousy.
Here's $15,000. If you need more, let me know.
Blank check enclosed. You fill it in. Whatever.
R. Chast

TRIAL BALLOONS IN APARTMENT 3-B
I've always wondered what it would be like to live on a boat in the Seventy-ninth Street Marina.
Jenny Witherspoon has a nose ring.
Rancid is playing at Irving Plaza next Thursday.
Lentils—a tasty, inexpensive alternative to meat.
R. Chast

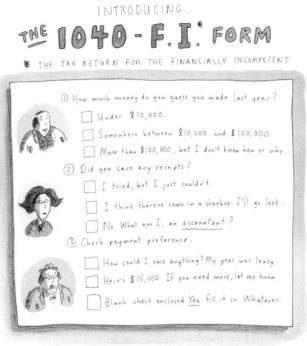

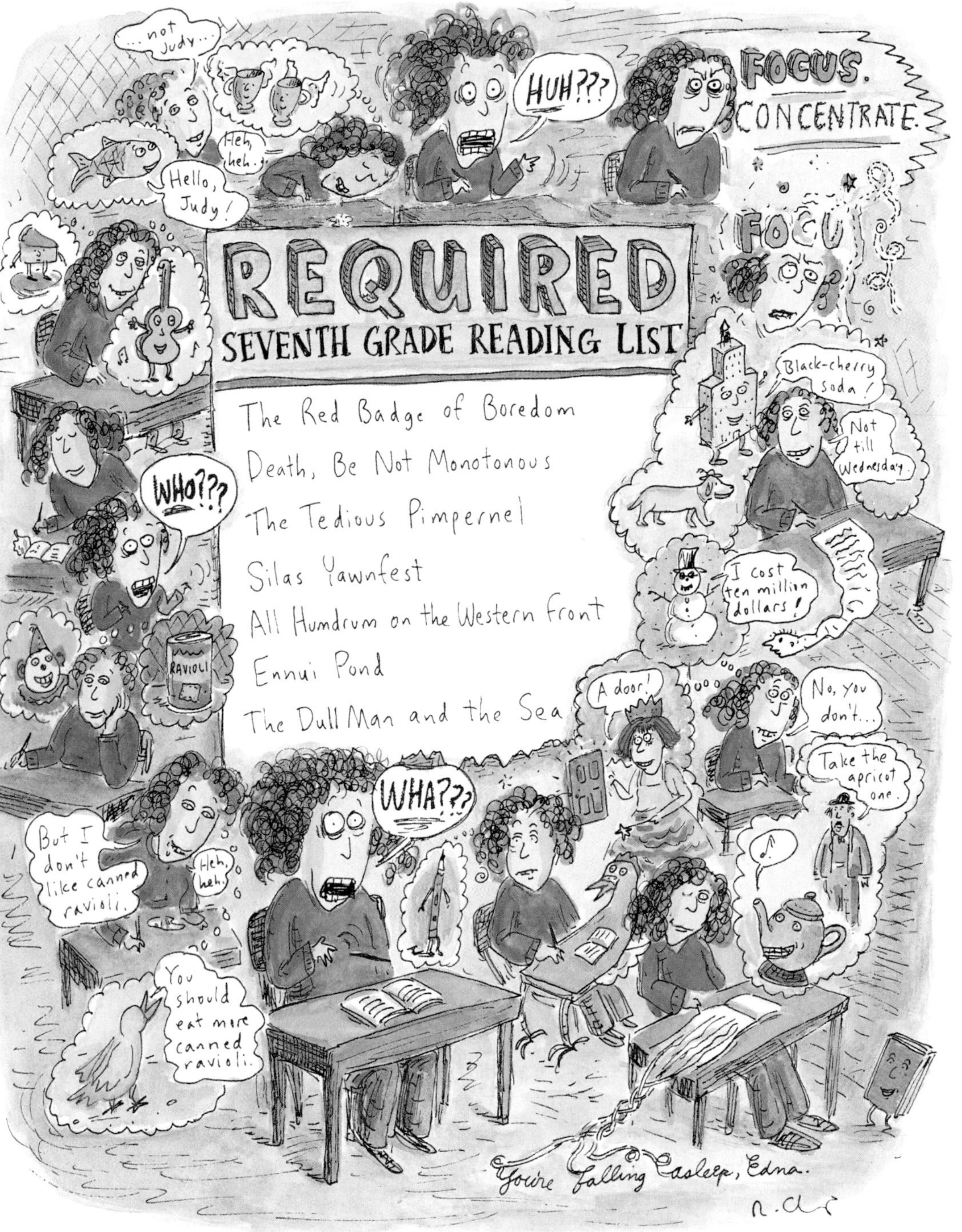

...not Judy...
Heh, heh.
HUH???
FOCUS.
CONCENTRATE.
Hello, Judy!
FOCU
REQUIRED
SEVENTH GRADE READING LIST
The Red Badge of Boredom
Death, Be Not Monotonous
The Tedious Pimpernel
Silas Yawnfest
All Humdrum on the Western Front
Ennui Pond
The Dull Man and the Sea
Black-cherry soda!
Not till Wednesday.
WHO???
I cost ten million dollars!
RAVIOLI
A door!
No, you don't...
Take the apricot one.
WHA???
But I don't like canned ravioli.
Heh, heh.
You should eat more canned ravioli.
You're falling asleep, Edna.
R. Ch

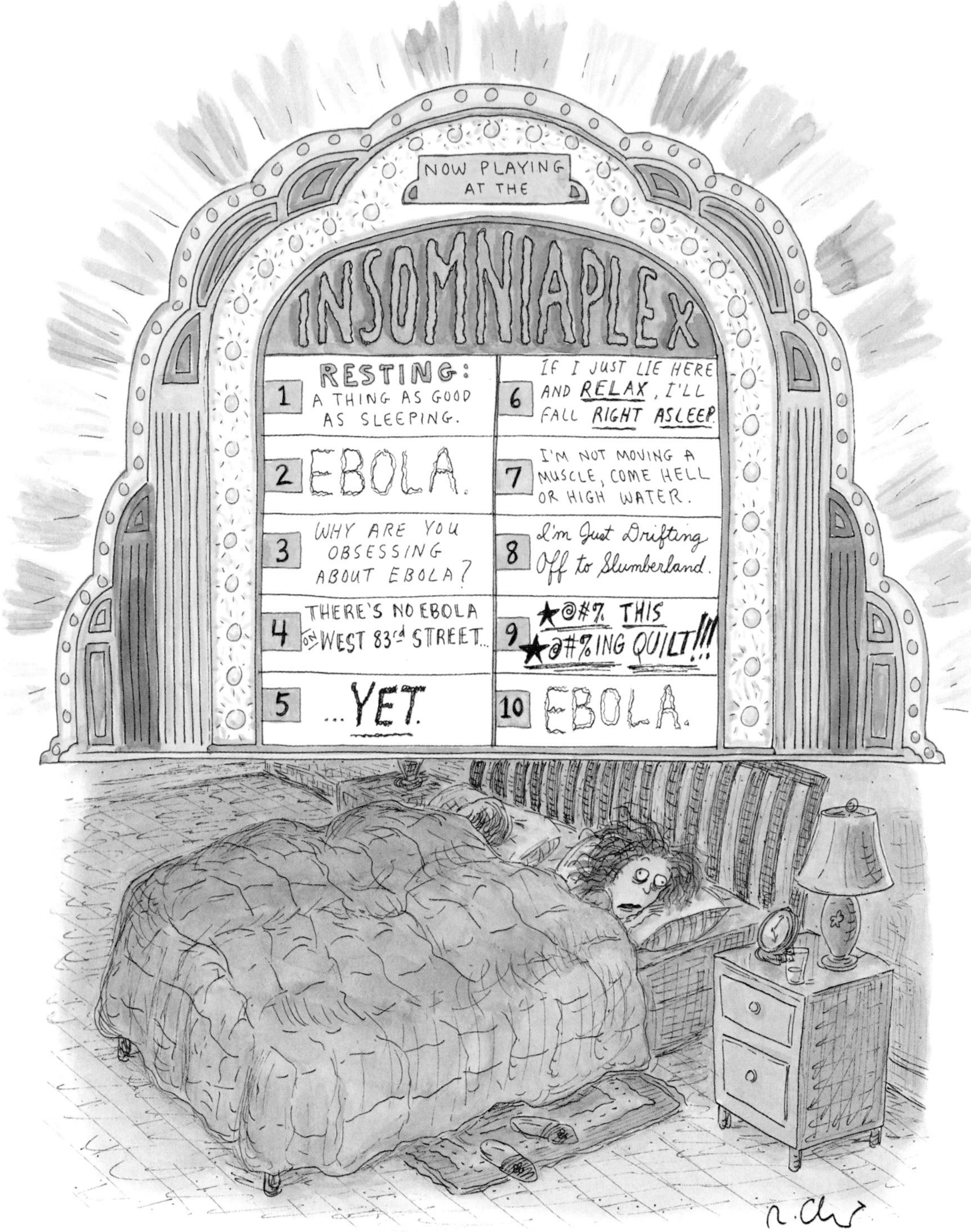
NOW PLAYING AT THE
INSOMNIAPLEX
1 RESTING: A THING AS GOOD AS SLEEPING.
2 EBOLA.
3 WHY ARE YOU OBSESSING ABOUT EBOLA?
4 THERE'S NO EBOLA ON WEST 83rd STREET...
5 ...YET.
6 IF I JUST LIE HERE AND RELAX, I'LL FALL RIGHT ASLEEP.
7 I'M NOT MOVING A MUSCLE, COME HELL OR HIGH WATER.
8 I'm Just Drifting Off to Slumberland.
9 ★@#% THIS ★@#%ING QUILT!!!
10 EBOLA.
R. Ch

HOAX ETHNIC FOOD

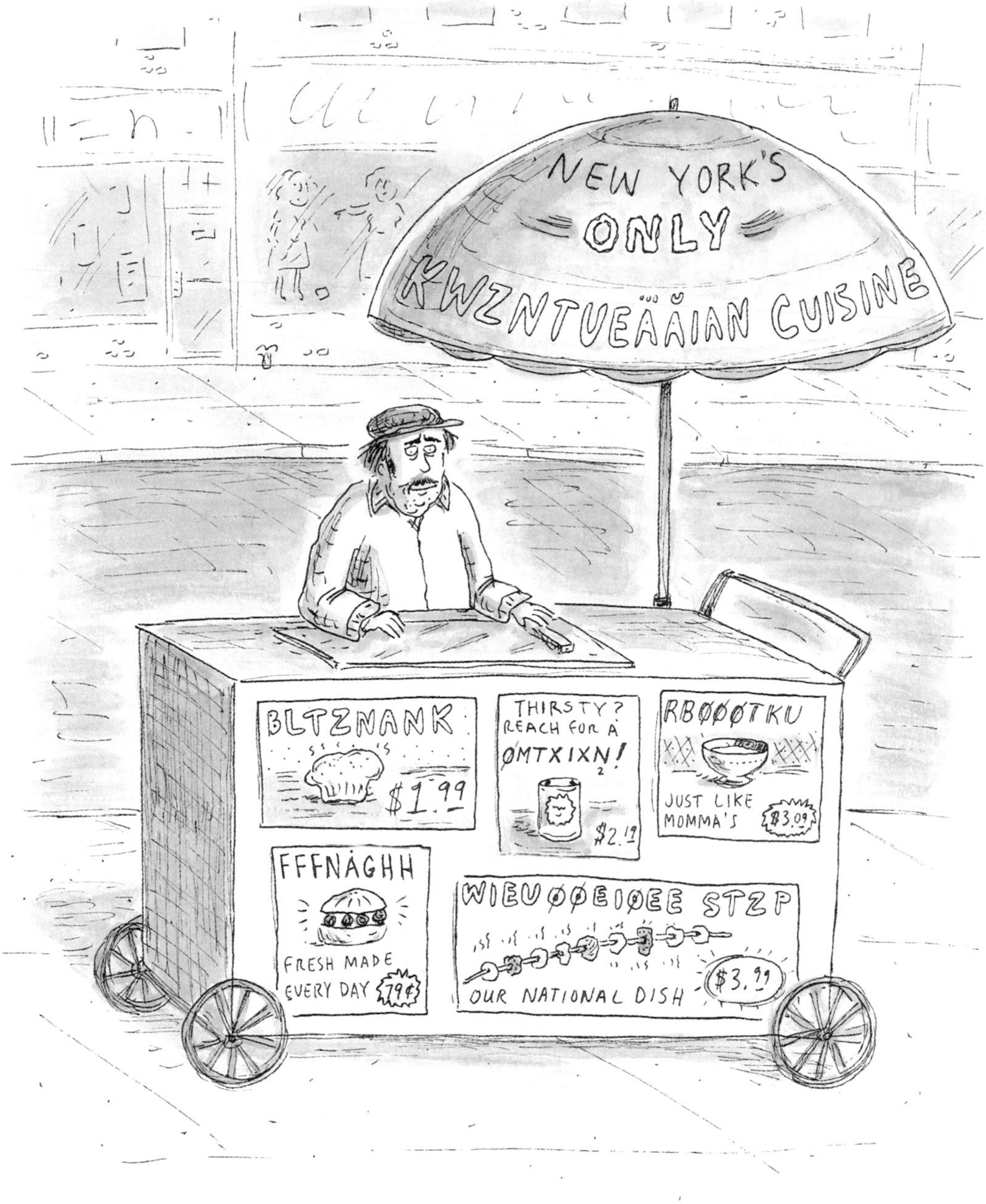
NEW YORK'S
ONLY
KWZNTUEÄĂIAN CUISINE
BLTZNANK
$1.99
THIRSTY? REACH FOR A ØMTXIXN!
$2.19
RBØØØTKU
JUST LIKE MOMMA'S
$3.09
FFFNAGHH
FRESH MADE EVERY DAY
79¢
WIEUØØEIØEE STZP
OUR NATIONAL DISH
$3.99

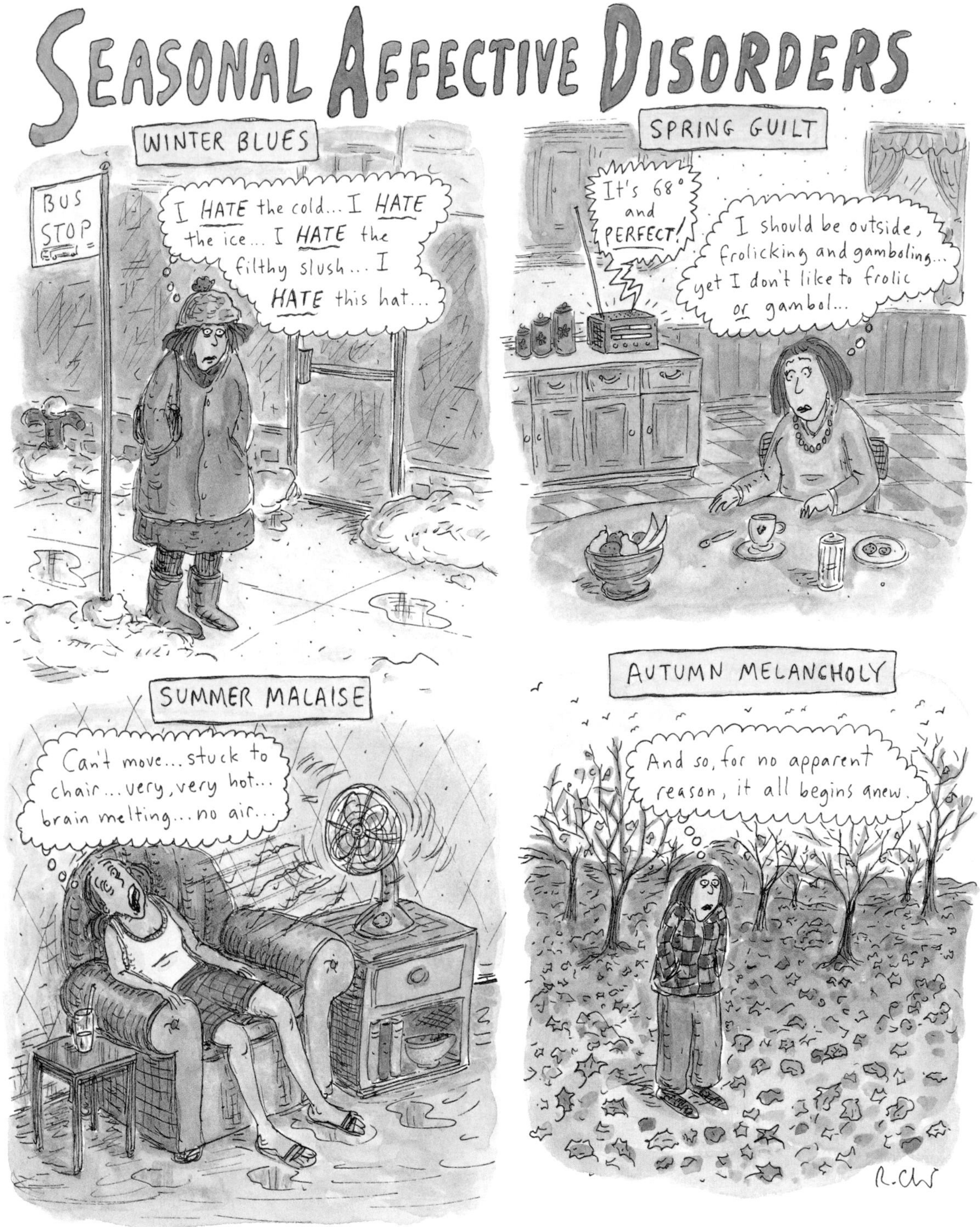
SEASONAL AFFECTIVE DISORDERS
WINTER BLUES
BUS STOP
I HATE the cold... I HATE the ice... I HATE the filthy slush... I HATE this hat...
SPRING GUILT
It's 68° and PERFECT!
I should be outside, frolicking and gamboling... yet I don't like to frolic or gambol...
SUMMER MALAISE
Can't move... stuck to chair... very, very hot... brain melting... no air...
AUTUMN MELANCHOLY
And so, for no apparent reason, it all begins anew.
R. Chast

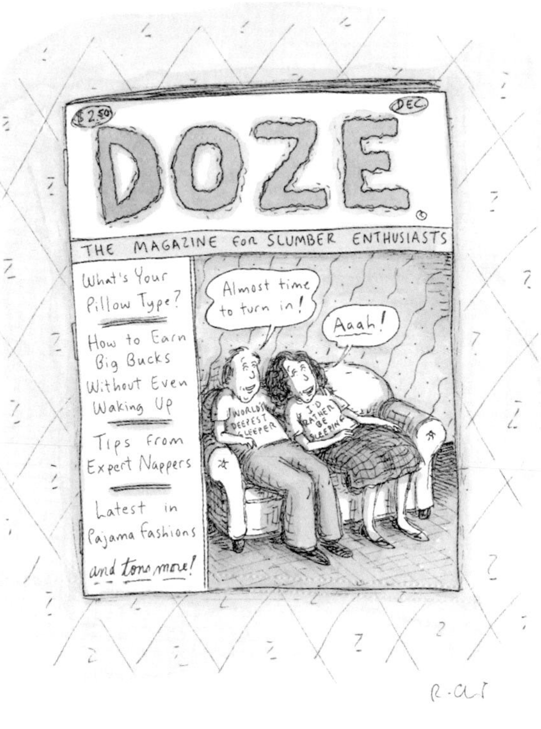
$2.50
DEC
DOZE
THE MAGAZINE for SLUMBER ENTHUSIASTS
What's Your Pillow Type?
How to Earn Big Bucks Without Even Waking Up
Tips from Expert Nappers
Latest in Pajama fashions
and tons more!
Almost time to turn in!
Aaah!
WORLD'S DEEPEST SLEEPER
I'D RATHER BE SLEEPING
R. Chast

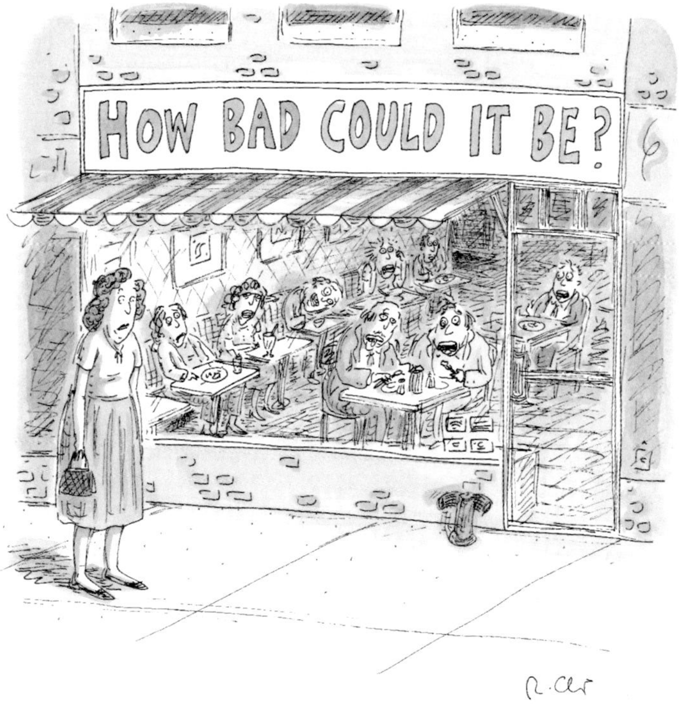
HOW BAD COULD IT BE?
R. Chast

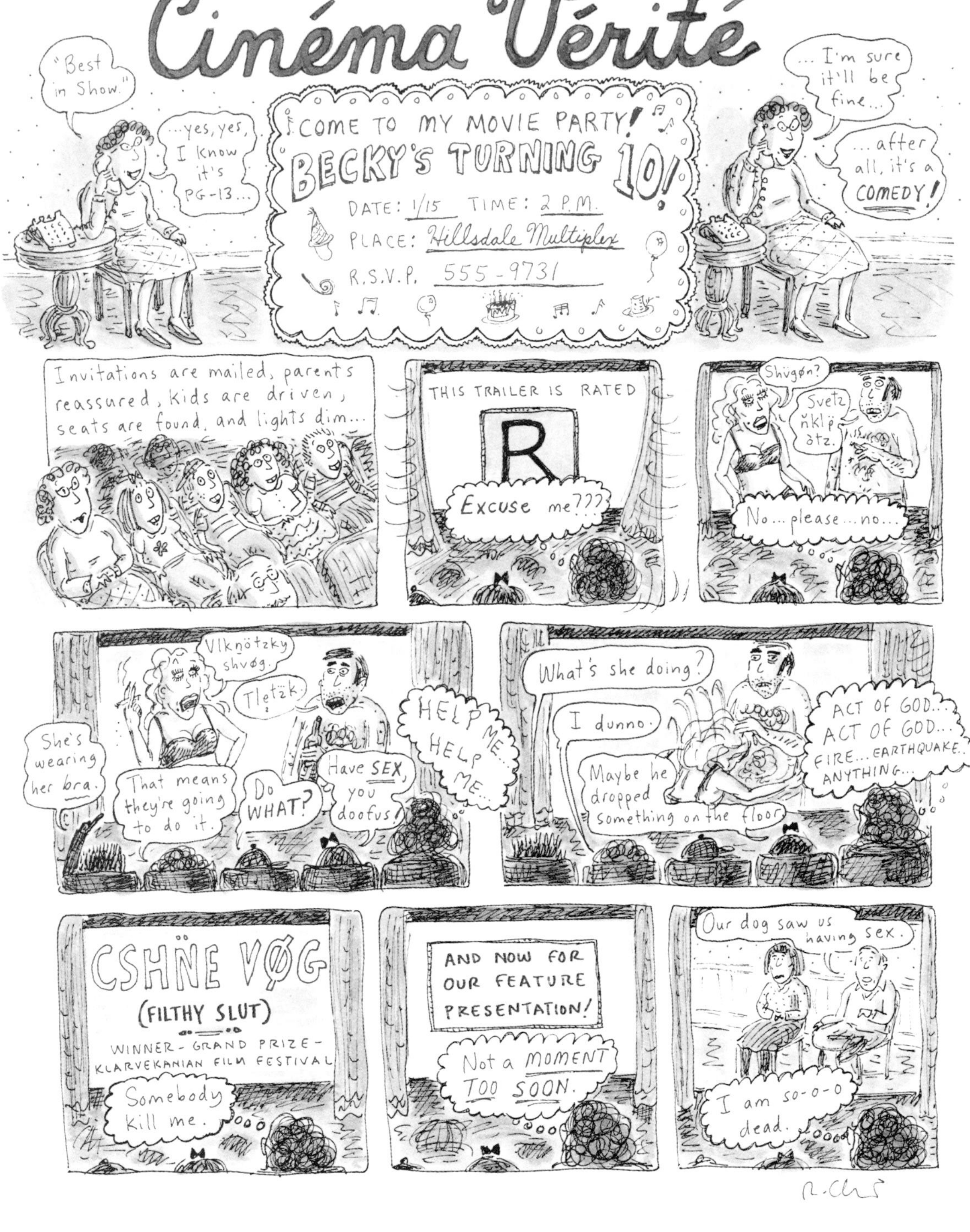
Cinéma Vérité
"Best in Show."
...yes, yes, I know it's PG-13...
COME TO MY MOVIE PARTY!
BECKY'S TURNING 10!
DATE: 1/15 TIME: 2 P.M.
PLACE: Hillsdale Multiplex
R.S.V.P. 555-9731
...I'm sure it'll be fine...
...after all, it's a COMEDY!
Invitations are mailed, parents reassured, kids are driven, seats are found, and lights dim...
THIS TRAILER IS RATED
R
Excuse me???
Shvgøn?
Svetz ňklp ötz.
No... please... no...
Vlknötzky shvøg.
Tletžk.
She's wearing her bra.
That means they're going to do it.
Do WHAT?
Have SEX, you doofus!
HELP ME... HELP ME...
What's she doing?
I dunno.
Maybe he dropped something on the floor.
ACT OF GOD... ACT OF GOD... FIRE... EARTHQUAKE... ANYTHING...
CSHÑE VØG
(FILTHY SLUT)
WINNER - GRAND PRIZE - KLARVEKANIAN FILM FESTIVAL
Somebody kill me.
AND NOW FOR OUR FEATURE PRESENTATION!
Not a MOMENT TOO SOON.
Our dog saw us having sex.
I am so-o-o dead.

RECIPES FOR COMFORT DRINKS

Cozy

2 oz. hot cocoa
4 oz. vodka
3 marshmallows

Combine cocoa and vodka. Garnish with marshmallows. Serves one nicely, but it's your call.

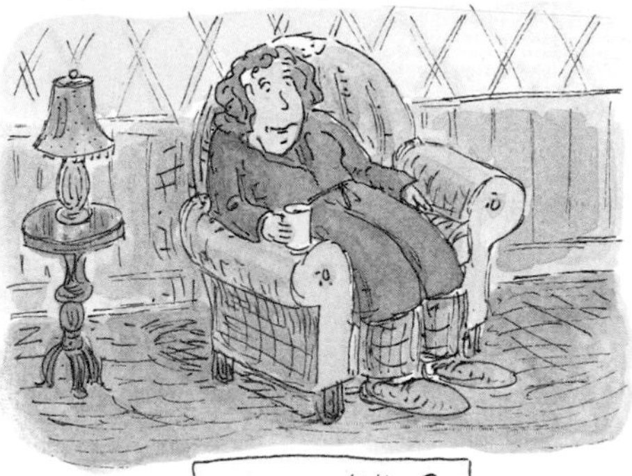

The Healing Begins

2 tbsp. hot milk
1 tbsp. honey
4 oz. rum

Stir everything together. Should be fine for one, but if a tad more is needed, that's O.K.

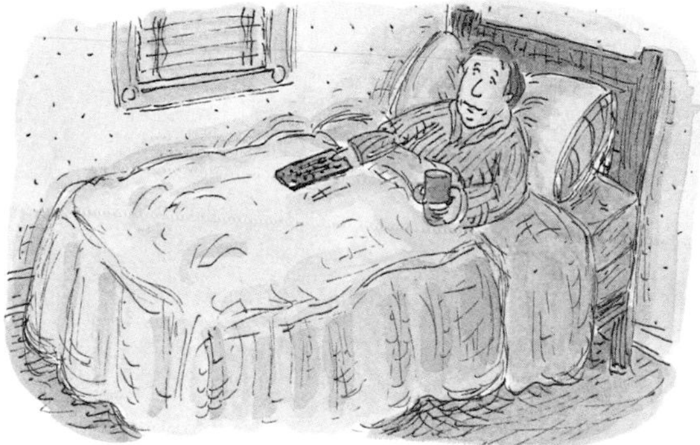

Osama *Who*?

1/2 c. camomile tea
2 tsp. sugar
4 oz. Scotch

Mix tea, sugar, and Scotch. Makes one, but, hey, who are we to say?

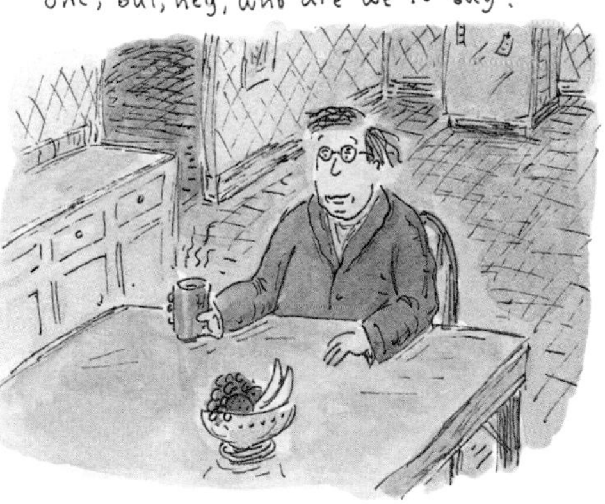

Home Security

1/2 c. vanilla pudding
4 oz. gin

Blend pudding and gin. One ought to do the trick, but these are difficult times.

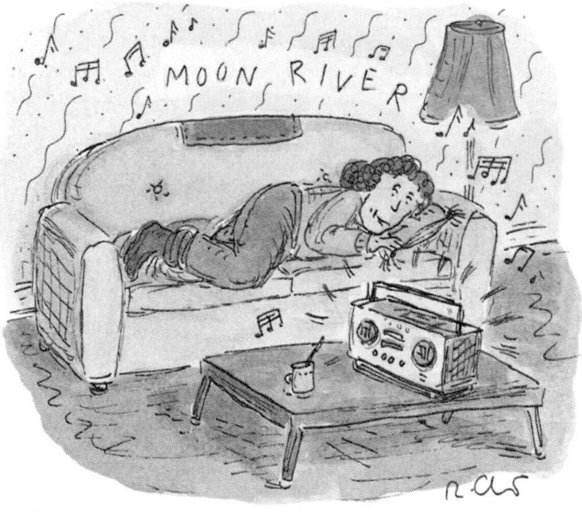
MOON RIVER
R.Ch

THE BERLITZ GUIDE TO

Flowerese

	Congratulations on your stomach-stapling.
	I like you— I'm just not <u>attracted</u> to you.
	Have a great time in Nebraska or whatever.
	I apologize for saying your parents were degenerates.
	Happy birthday! It must feel weird to be sixty.

R.Ch

FIRST-PERIOD ALGEBRA

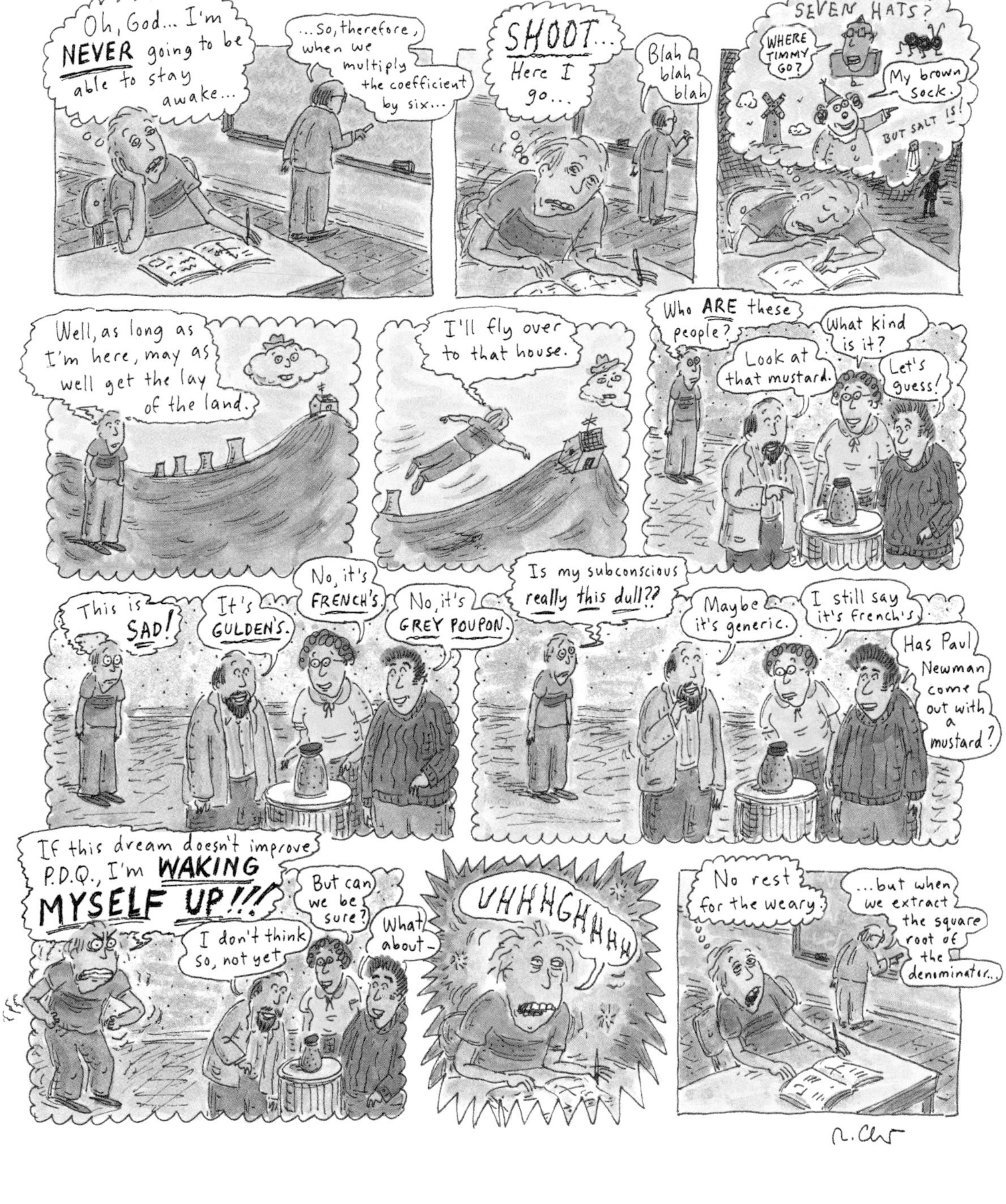

Oh, God... I'm NEVER going to be able to stay awake...
...So, therefore, when we multiply the coefficient by six...
SHOOT... Here I go...
Blah blah blah
SEVEN HATS?
WHERE TIMMY GO?
My brown sock.
BUT SALT IS!
Well, as long as I'm here, may as well get the lay of the land.
I'll fly over to that house.
Who ARE these people?
Look at that mustard.
What kind is it?
Let's guess!
This is SAD!
It's GULDEN'S.
No, it's FRENCH'S.
No, it's GREY POUPON.
Is my subconscious really this dull??
Maybe it's generic.
I still say it's French's.
Has Paul Newman come out with a mustard?
If this dream doesn't improve P.D.Q., I'm WAKING MYSELF UP!!!
I don't think so, not yet
But can we be sure?
What about-
UHHHGHHHH
No rest for the weary.
...but when we extract the square root of the denominator...

DREAM PARENTS

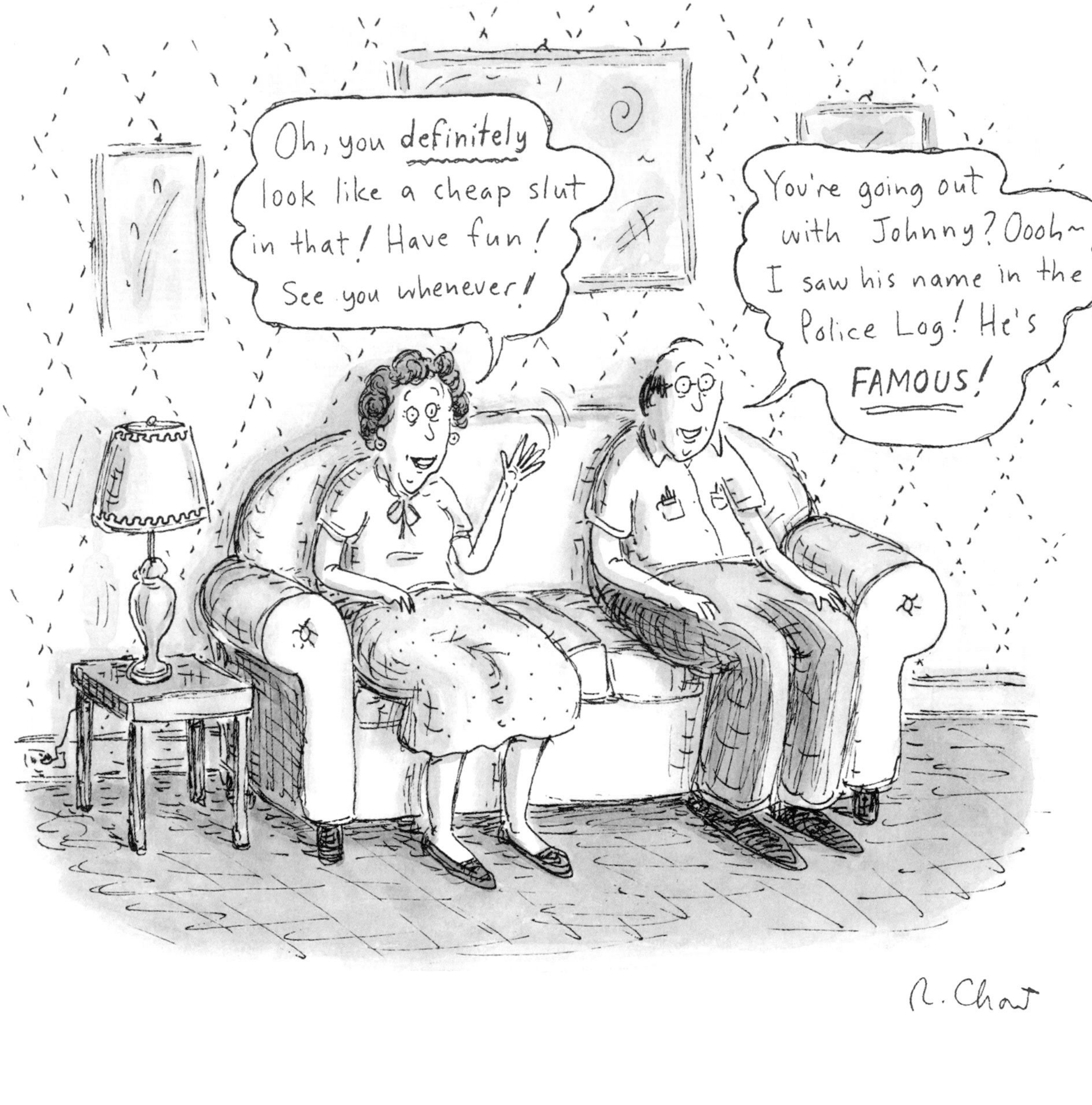
Oh, you definitely look like a cheap slut in that! Have fun! See you whenever!
You're going out with Johnny? Oooh~ I saw his name in the Police Log! He's FAMOUS!
R. Chast

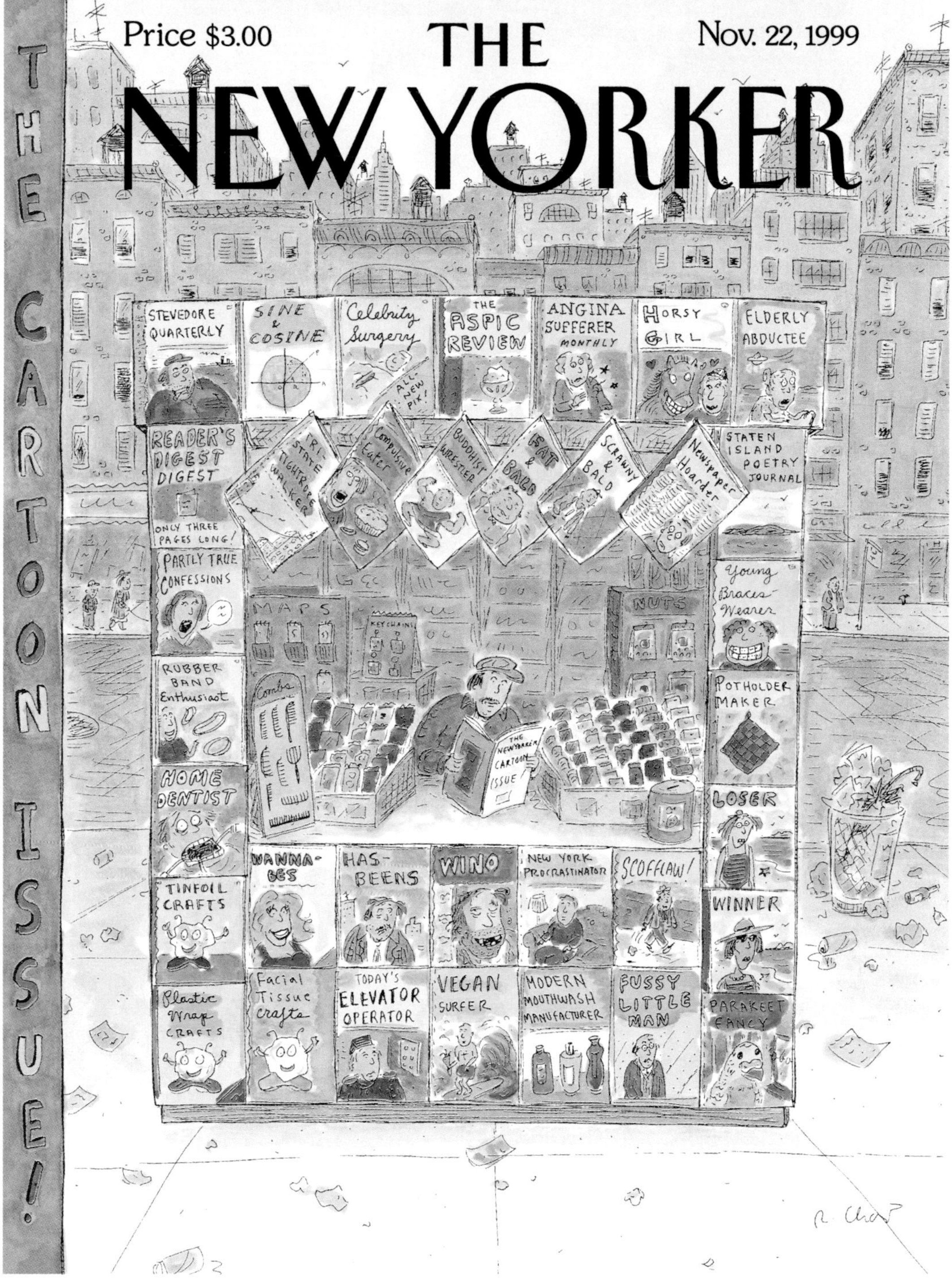
Price $3.00
THE NEW YORKER
Nov. 22, 1999
THE CARTOON ISSUE!
STEVEDORE QUARTERLY
SINE & COSINE
Celebrity Surgery
ALL NEW PIX!
THE ASPIC REVIEW
ANGINA SUFFERER MONTHLY
HORSY GIRL
ELDERLY ABDUCTEE
READER'S DIGEST DIGEST
ONLY THREE PAGES LONG!
TRI-STATE TIGHTROPE WALKER
Compulsive Eater
Buddhist Wrestler
FAT & BALD
SCRAWNY & BALD
Newspaper Hoarder
STATEN ISLAND POETRY JOURNAL
PARTLY TRUE CONFESSIONS
MAPS
KEYCHAINS
NUTS
Young Braces-Wearer
RUBBER BAND Enthusiast
Combs
THE NEW YORKER CARTOON ISSUE
POTHOLDER MAKER
HOME DENTIST
LOSER
WANNA-BES
HAS-BEENS
WINO
NEW YORK PROCRASTINATOR
SCOFFLAW!
TINFOIL CRAFTS
WINNER
Plastic Wrap CRAFTS
Facial Tissue crafts
TODAY'S ELEVATOR OPERATOR
VEGAN SURFER
MODERN MOUTHWASH MANUFACTURER
FUSSY LITTLE MAN
PARAKEET FANCY

NANCY DREW MYSTERIES
THE LATER YEARS
NANCY DREW AND THE MISSING HOUSE KEYS
I know I left them RIGHT THERE.
NANCY DREW AND THE MYSTERY OF THE EIGHT POUNDS
How did I gain eight pounds? I eat nothing!
NANCY DREW AND THE SECRET OF THE COMPUTER
You and I are going to be GREAT FRIENDS!
R. Chast

THE BULL, THE BEAR, THE ANT, AND THE GRASSHOPPER
Stocks, my friend. Now is the time.
I dunno. I'd hedge my bets a little, do a few bonds.
Excuse me, but hasn't anybody ever heard the words "SAVINGS ACCOUNT"?
Let's stop talking about money and go have some FUN!
R. Chast

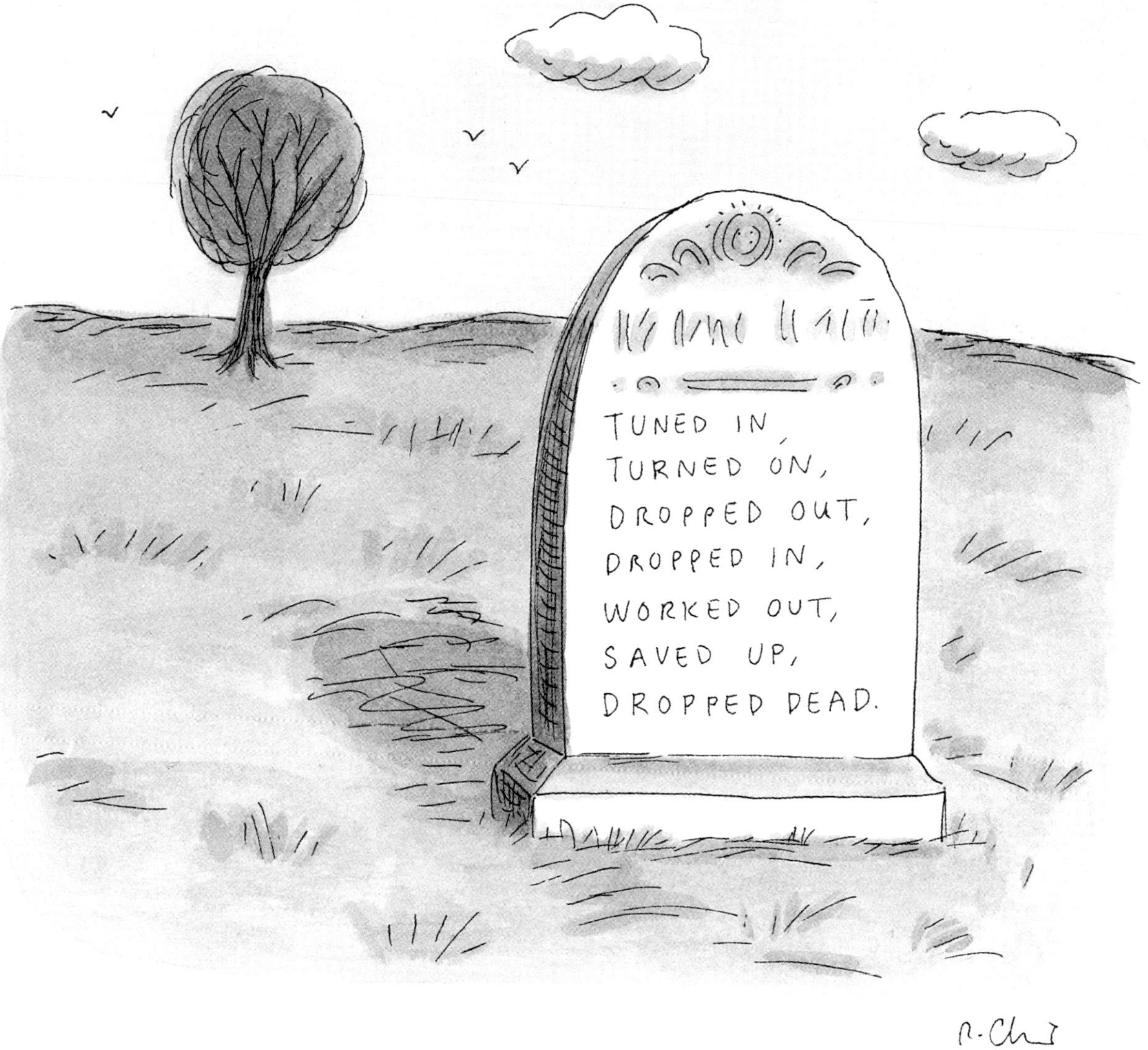
TUNED IN,
TURNED ON,
DROPPED OUT,
DROPPED IN,
WORKED OUT,
SAVED UP,
DROPPED DEAD.
R. Chast

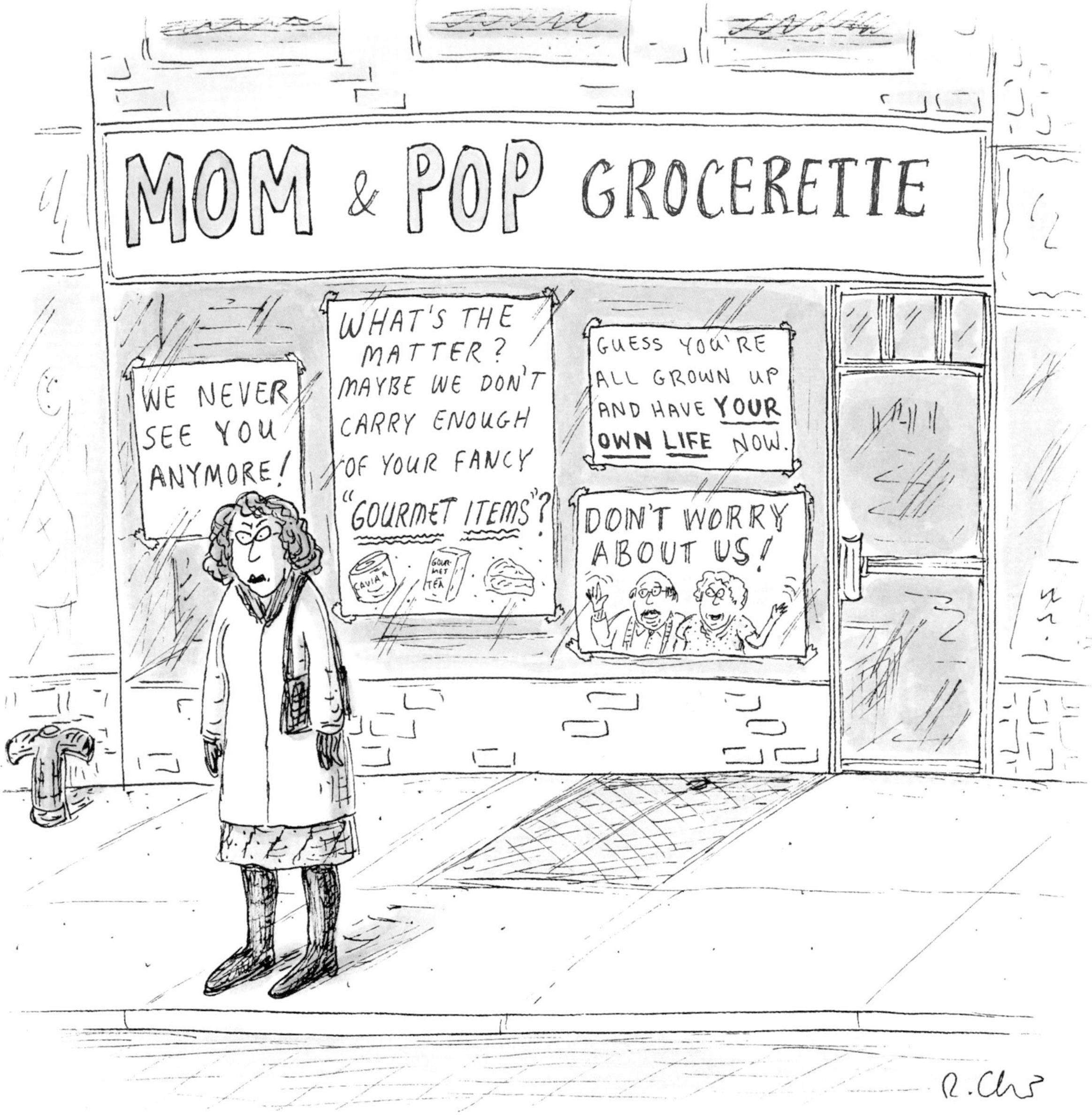
MOM & POP GROCERETTE
WE NEVER SEE YOU ANYMORE!
WHAT'S THE MATTER? MAYBE WE DON'T CARRY ENOUGH OF YOUR FANCY "GOURMET ITEMS"?
CAVIAR
GOURMET TEA
GUESS YOU'RE ALL GROWN UP AND HAVE YOUR OWN LIFE NOW.
DON'T WORRY ABOUT US!
R. Chast

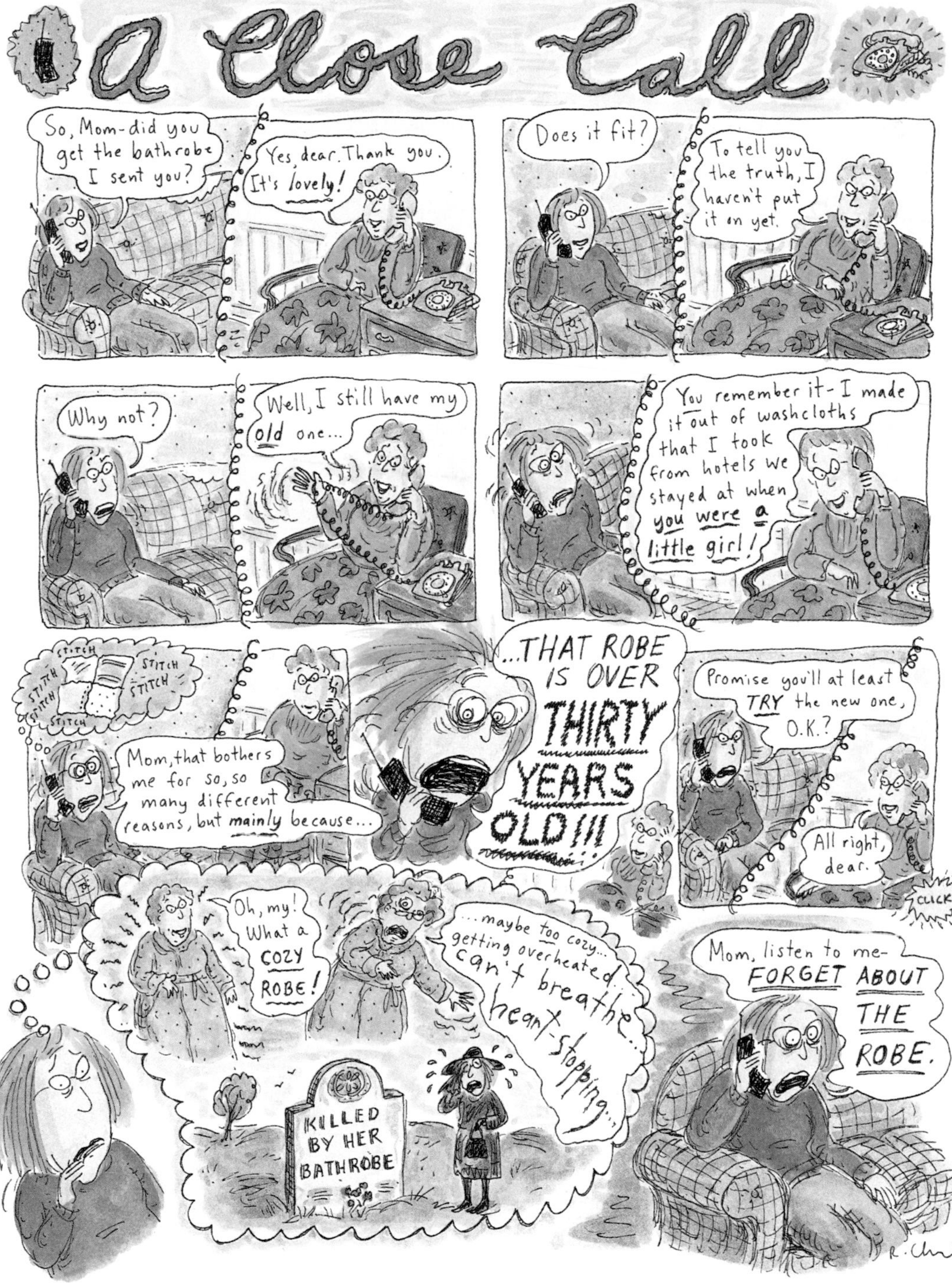
A Close Call
So, Mom-did you get the bathrobe I sent you?
Yes, dear. Thank you. It's lovely!
Does it fit?
To tell you the truth, I haven't put it on yet.
Why not?
Well, I still have my old one...
You remember it-I made it out of washcloths that I took from hotels we stayed at when you were a little girl!
STITCH STITCH STITCH STITCH STITCH
Mom, that bothers me for so, so many different reasons, but mainly because...
...THAT ROBE IS OVER THIRTY YEARS OLD!!!
Promise you'll at least TRY the new one, O.K.?
All right, dear.
CLICK
Oh, my! What a COZY ROBE!
...maybe too cozy... getting overheated... can't breathe... heart-stopping...
KILLED BY HER BATHROBE
Mom, listen to me-FORGET ABOUT THE ROBE.
R. Chast

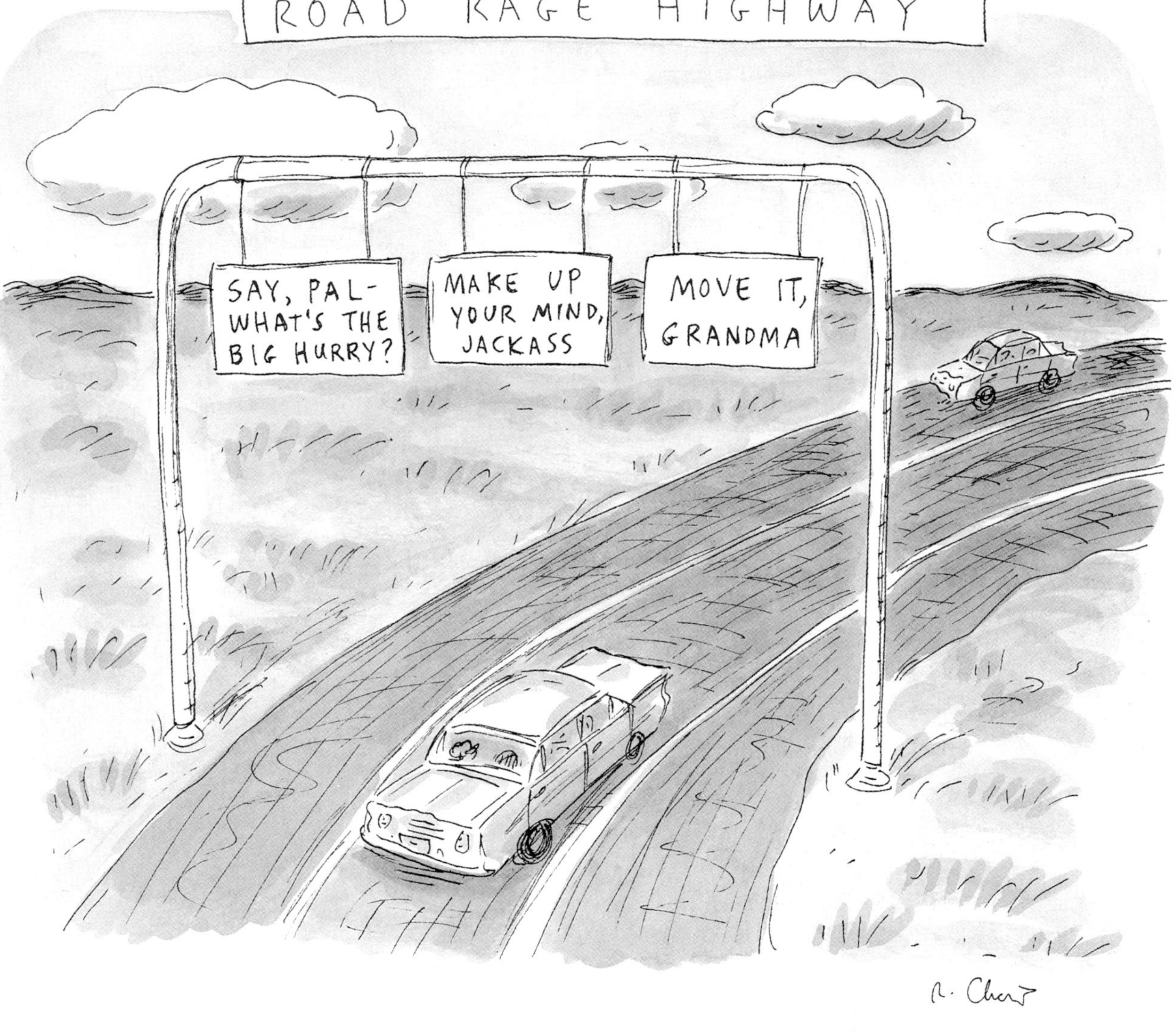
ROAD RAGE HIGHWAY
SAY, PAL- WHAT'S THE BIG HURRY?
MAKE UP YOUR MIND, JACKASS
MOVE IT, GRANDMA
R. Chast

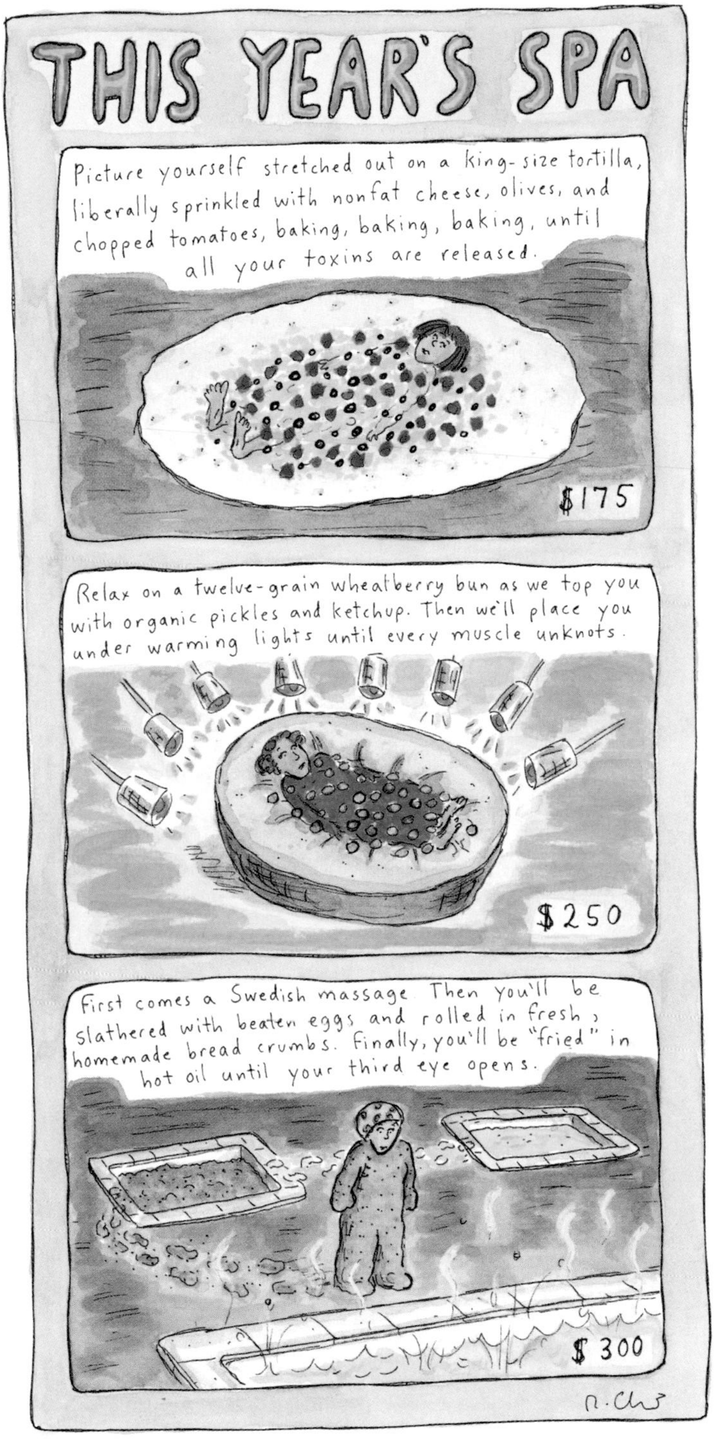
THIS YEAR'S SPA
Picture yourself stretched out on a king-size tortilla, liberally sprinkled with nonfat cheese, olives, and chopped tomatoes, baking, baking, baking, until all your toxins are released.
$175
Relax on a twelve-grain wheatberry bun as we top you with organic pickles and ketchup. Then we'll place you under warming lights until every muscle unknots.
$250
First comes a Swedish massage. Then you'll be slathered with beaten eggs and rolled in fresh, homemade bread crumbs. Finally, you'll be "fried" in hot oil until your third eye opens.
$300
R. Chast

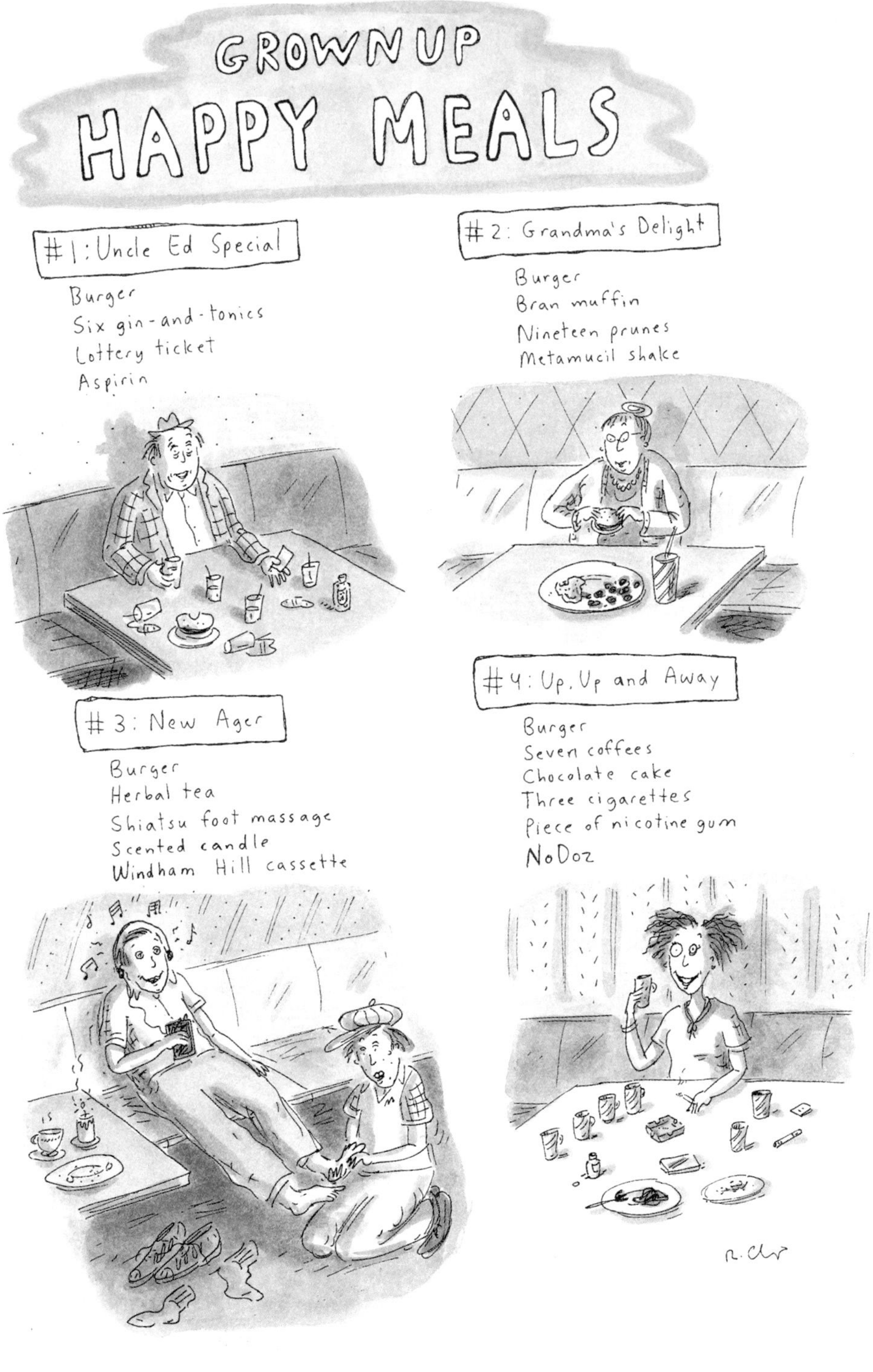
GROWNUP
HAPPY MEALS
#1: Uncle Ed Special
Burger
Six gin-and-tonics
Lottery ticket
Aspirin
#2: Grandma's Delight
Burger
Bran muffin
Nineteen prunes
Metamucil shake
#3: New Ager
Burger
Herbal tea
Shiatsu foot massage
Scented candle
Windham Hill cassette
#4: Up, Up and Away
Burger
Seven coffees
Chocolate cake
Three cigarettes
Piece of nicotine gum
NoDoz

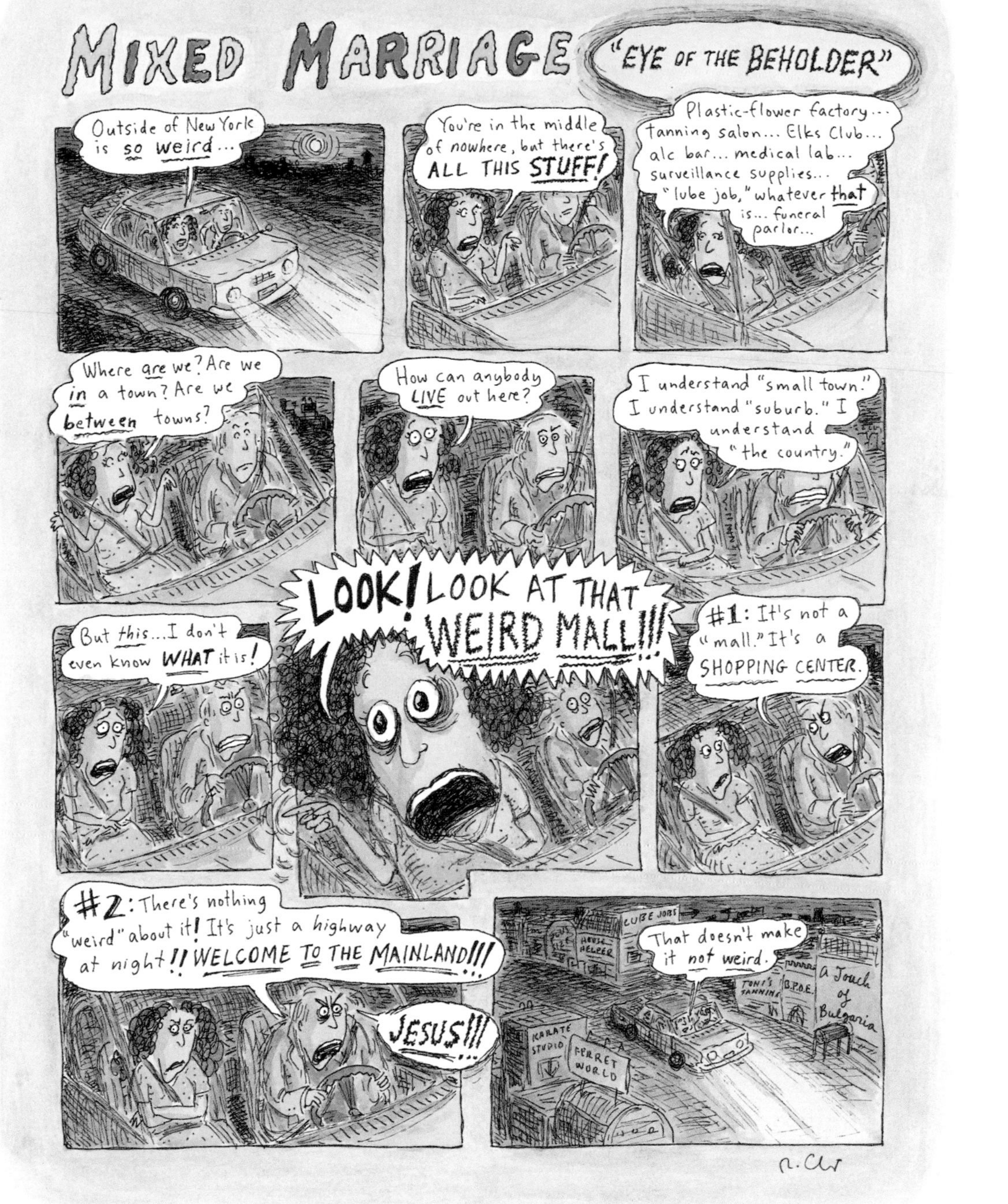
MIXED MARRIAGE
"EYE OF THE BEHOLDER"
Outside of New York is so weird...
You're in the middle of nowhere, but there's ALL THIS STUFF!
Plastic-flower factory... tanning salon... Elks Club... alc bar... medical lab... surveillance supplies... "lube job," whatever that is... funeral parlor...
Where are we? Are we in a town? Are we between towns?
How can anybody LIVE out here?
I understand "small town." I understand "suburb." I understand "the country."
But this... I don't even know WHAT it is!
LOOK! LOOK AT THAT WEIRD MALL!!!
#1: It's not a "mall." It's a SHOPPING CENTER.
#2: There's nothing "weird" about it! It's just a highway at night!! WELCOME TO THE MAINLAND!!!
JESUS!!!
LUBE JOBS
HOUSE HELPER
That doesn't make it not weird.
TONI'S TANNING
B.P.O.E.
A Touch of Bulgaria
KARATE STUDIO
FERRET WORLD
R. Chr

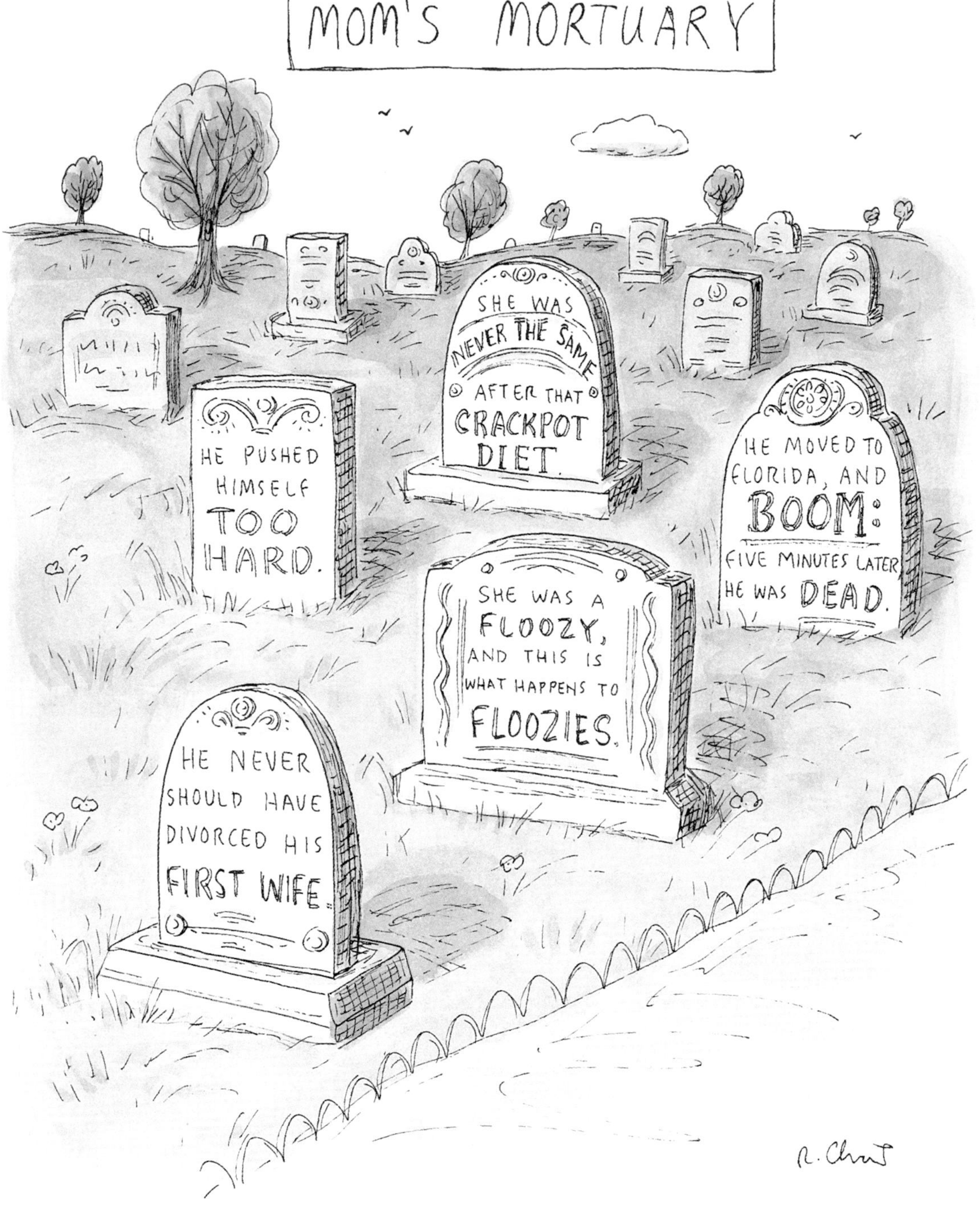
MOM'S MORTUARY
SHE WAS NEVER THE SAME AFTER THAT CRACKPOT DIET.
HE PUSHED HIMSELF TOO HARD.
HE MOVED TO FLORIDA, AND BOOM: FIVE MINUTES LATER HE WAS DEAD.
SHE WAS A FLOOZY, AND THIS IS WHAT HAPPENS TO FLOOZIES.
HE NEVER SHOULD HAVE DIVORCED HIS FIRST WIFE.
R. Chast

$3
JULY
Schadenfreude
MONTHLY
Guess Who's Bankrupt?
No-Talent Ho's Movie Bombs BIG TIME!
Notorious Brown-Nosing Hack's Book Gets Terrible Reviews!
and plenty more!
OBNOXIOUS HEIRESS'S COSMETIC SURGERY GOES HORRIBLY WRONG!
SCADS OF GRUESOME PICTURES, pages 11-15
R. Chast

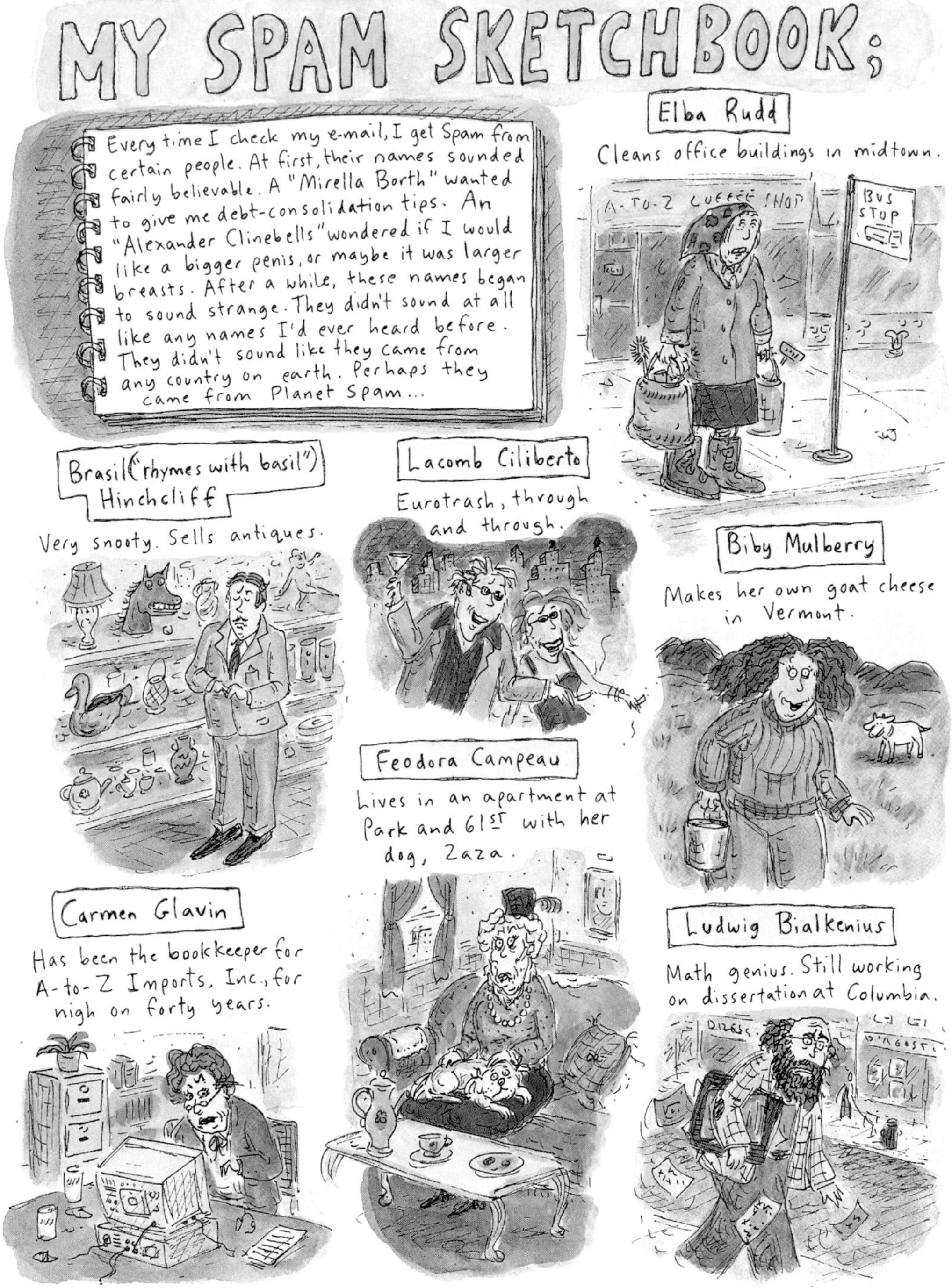
MY SPAM SKETCHBOOK:
Every time I check my e-mail, I get Spam from certain people. At first, their names sounded fairly believable. A "Mirella Borth" wanted to give me debt-consolidation tips. An "Alexander Clinebells" wondered if I would like a bigger penis, or maybe it was larger breasts. After a while, these names began to sound strange. They didn't sound at all like any names I'd ever heard before. They didn't sound like they came from any country on earth. Perhaps they came from Planet Spam...
Elba Rudd
Cleans office buildings in midtown.
A-TO-Z COFFEE SHOP
BUS STOP
Brasil ("rhymes with basil") Hinchcliff
Very snooty. Sells antiques.
Lacomb Ciliberto
Eurotrash, through and through.
Biby Mulberry
Makes her own goat cheese in Vermont.
Feodora Campeau
Lives in an apartment at Park and 61st with her dog, Zaza.
Carmen Glavin
Has been the bookkeeper for A-to-Z Imports, Inc., for nigh on forty years.
Ludwig Bialkenius
Math genius. Still working on dissertation at Columbia.

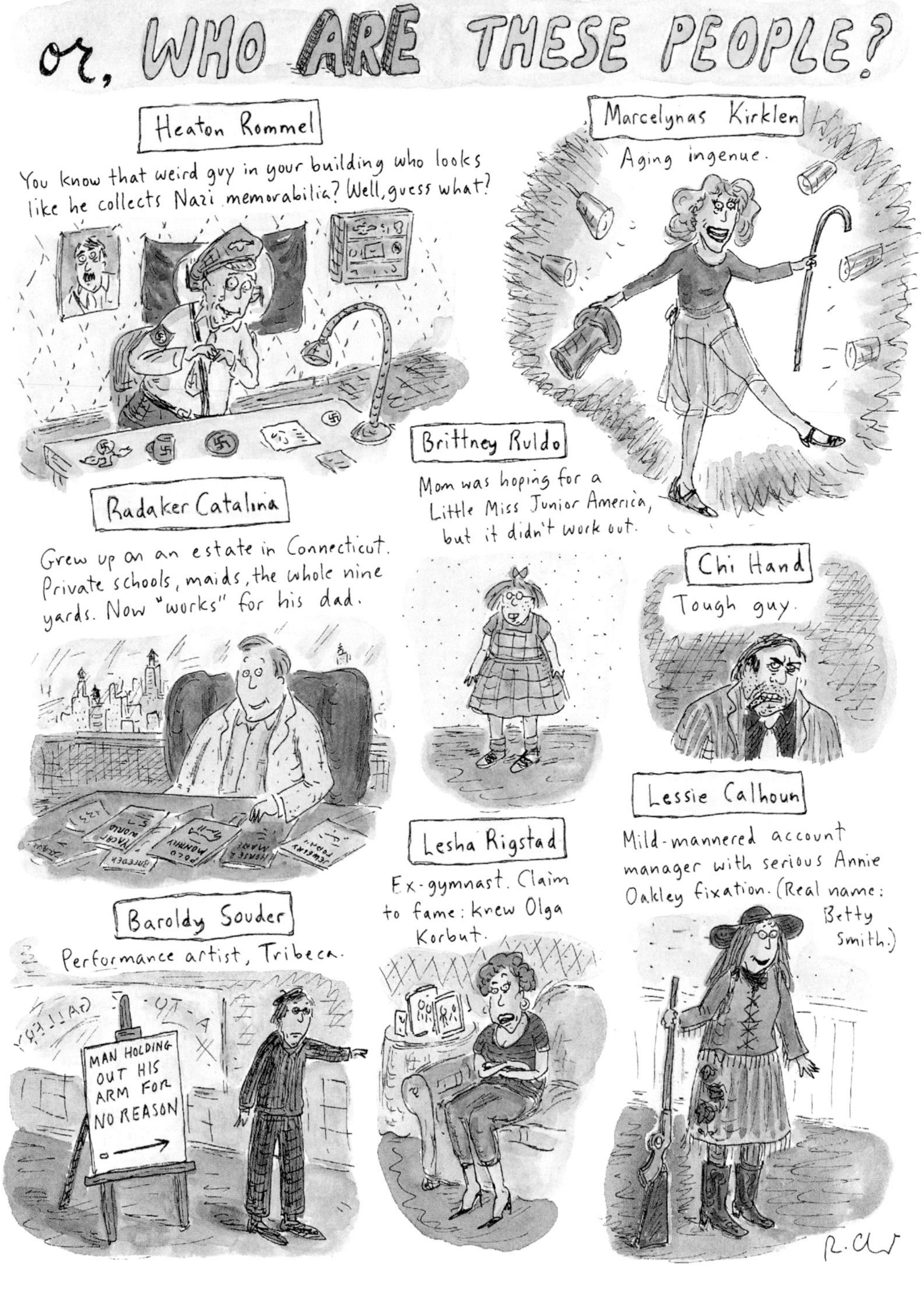

or, WHO ARE THESE PEOPLE?
Heaton Rommel
You know that weird guy in your building who looks like he collects Nazi memorabilia? Well, guess what?
Marcelynas Kirklen
Aging ingenue.
Radaker Catalina
Grew up on an estate in Connecticut. Private schools, maids, the whole nine yards. Now "works" for his dad.
Brittney Ruldo
Mom was hoping for a Little Miss Junior America, but it didn't work out.
Chi Hand
Tough guy.
Lessie Calhoun
Mild-mannered account manager with serious Annie Oakley fixation. (Real name: Betty Smith.)
Lesha Rigstad
Ex-gymnast. Claim to fame: knew Olga Korbut.
Baroldy Souder
Performance artist, Tribeca.
MAN HOLDING OUT HIS ARM FOR NO REASON

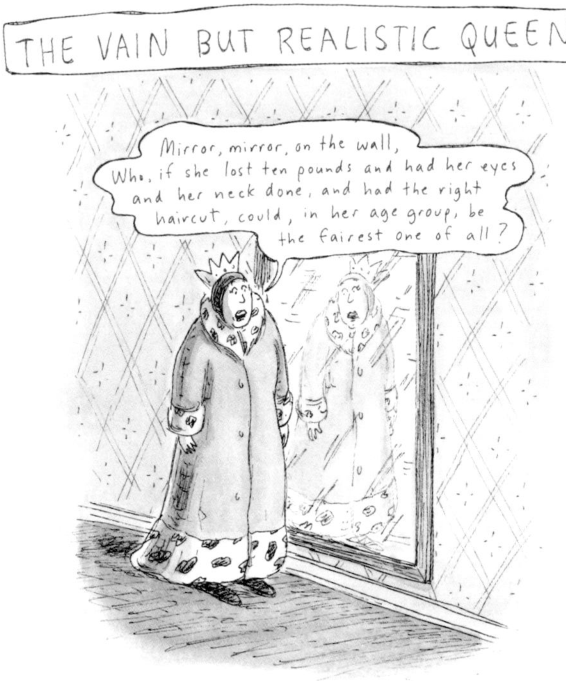
THE VAIN BUT REALISTIC QUEEN
Mirror, mirror, on the wall, Who, if she lost ten pounds and had her eyes and her neck done, and had the right haircut, could, in her age group, be the fairest one of all?

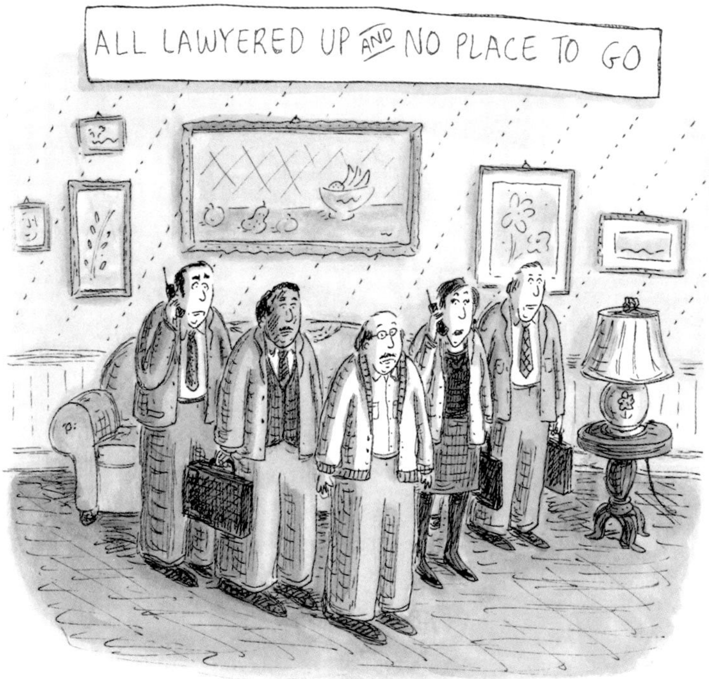
ALL LAWYERED UP AND NO PLACE TO GO

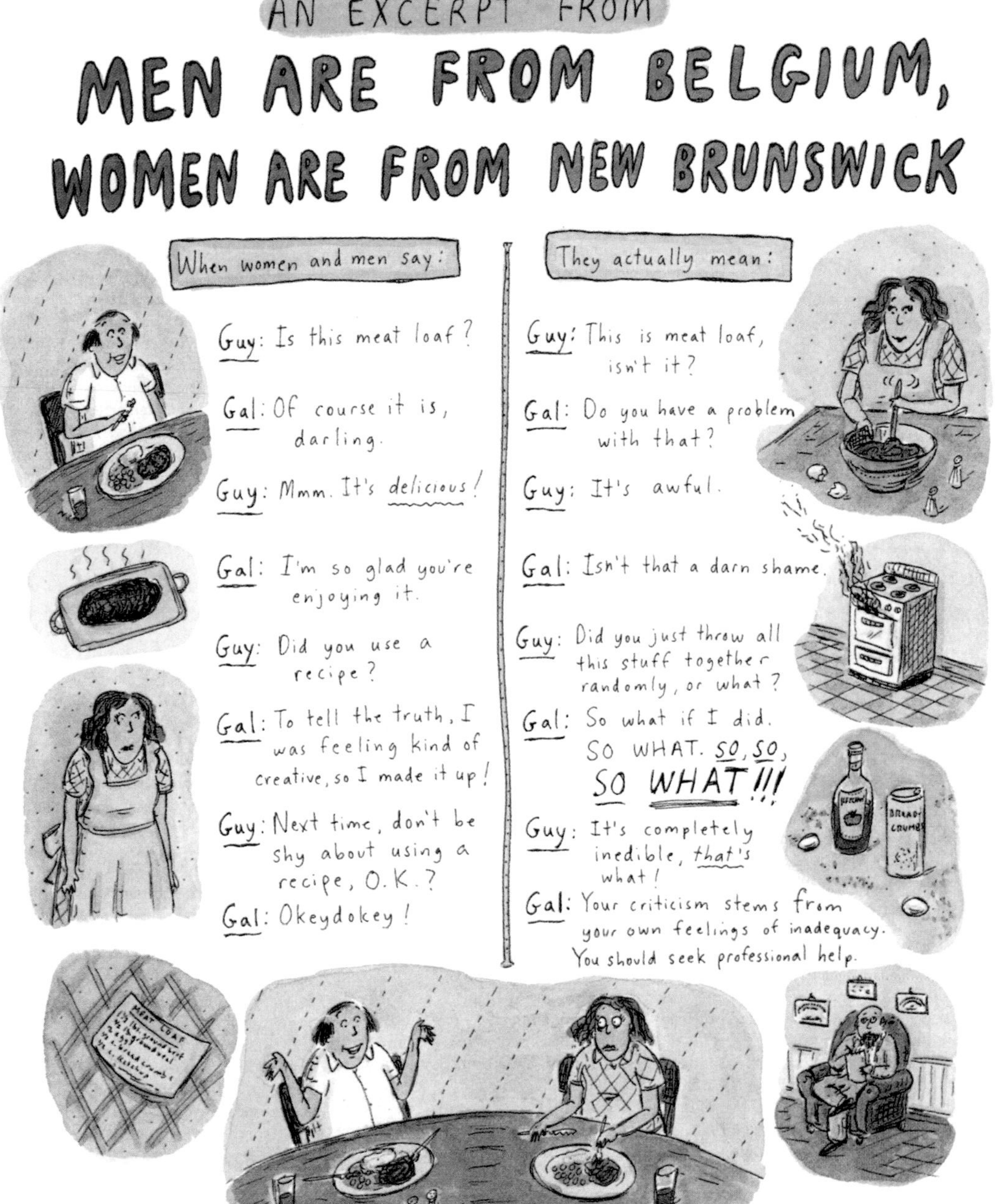
AN EXCERPT FROM
MEN ARE FROM BELGIUM, WOMEN ARE FROM NEW BRUNSWICK
When women and men say:
Guy: Is this meat loaf?
Gal: Of course it is, darling.
Guy: Mmm. It's delicious!
Gal: I'm so glad you're enjoying it.
Guy: Did you use a recipe?
Gal: To tell the truth, I was feeling kind of creative, so I made it up!
Guy: Next time, don't be shy about using a recipe, O.K.?
Gal: Okeydokey!
They actually mean:
Guy: This is meat loaf, isn't it?
Gal: Do you have a problem with that?
Guy: It's awful.
Gal: Isn't that a darn shame.
Guy: Did you just throw all this stuff together randomly, or what?
Gal: So what if I did. SO WHAT. SO, SO, SO WHAT!!!
Guy: It's completely inedible, that's what!
Gal: Your criticism stems from your own feelings of inadequacy. You should seek professional help.
MEAT LOAF
BREAD CRUMBS

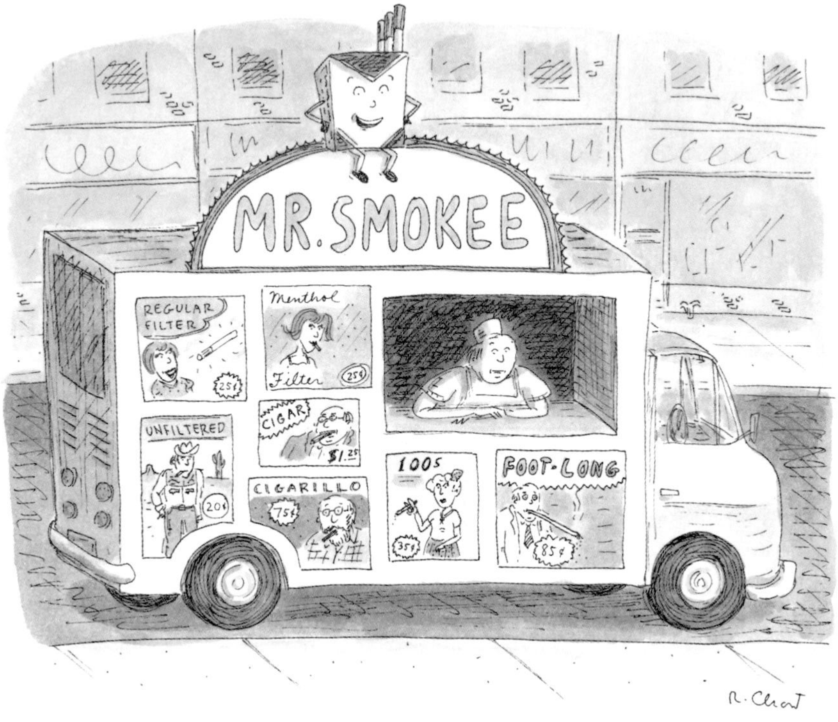
MR. SMOKEE
REGULAR FILTER
25¢
Menthol Filter
25¢
UNFILTERED
20¢
CIGAR
$1.25
CIGARILLO
75¢
100s
35¢
FOOT-LONG
85¢

THREE-WAY MIRROR

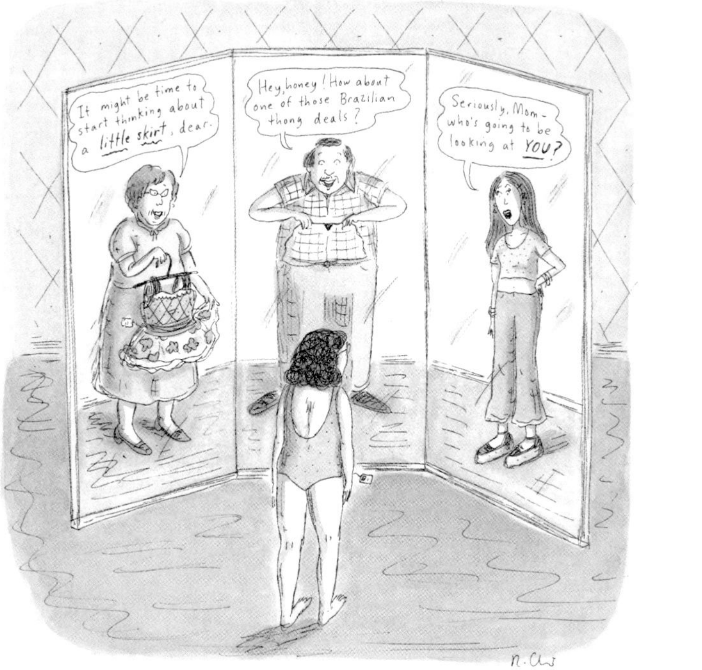
It might be time to start thinking about a little skirt, dear.
Hey, honey! How about one of those Brazilian thong deals?
Seriously, Mom—who's going to be looking at YOU?

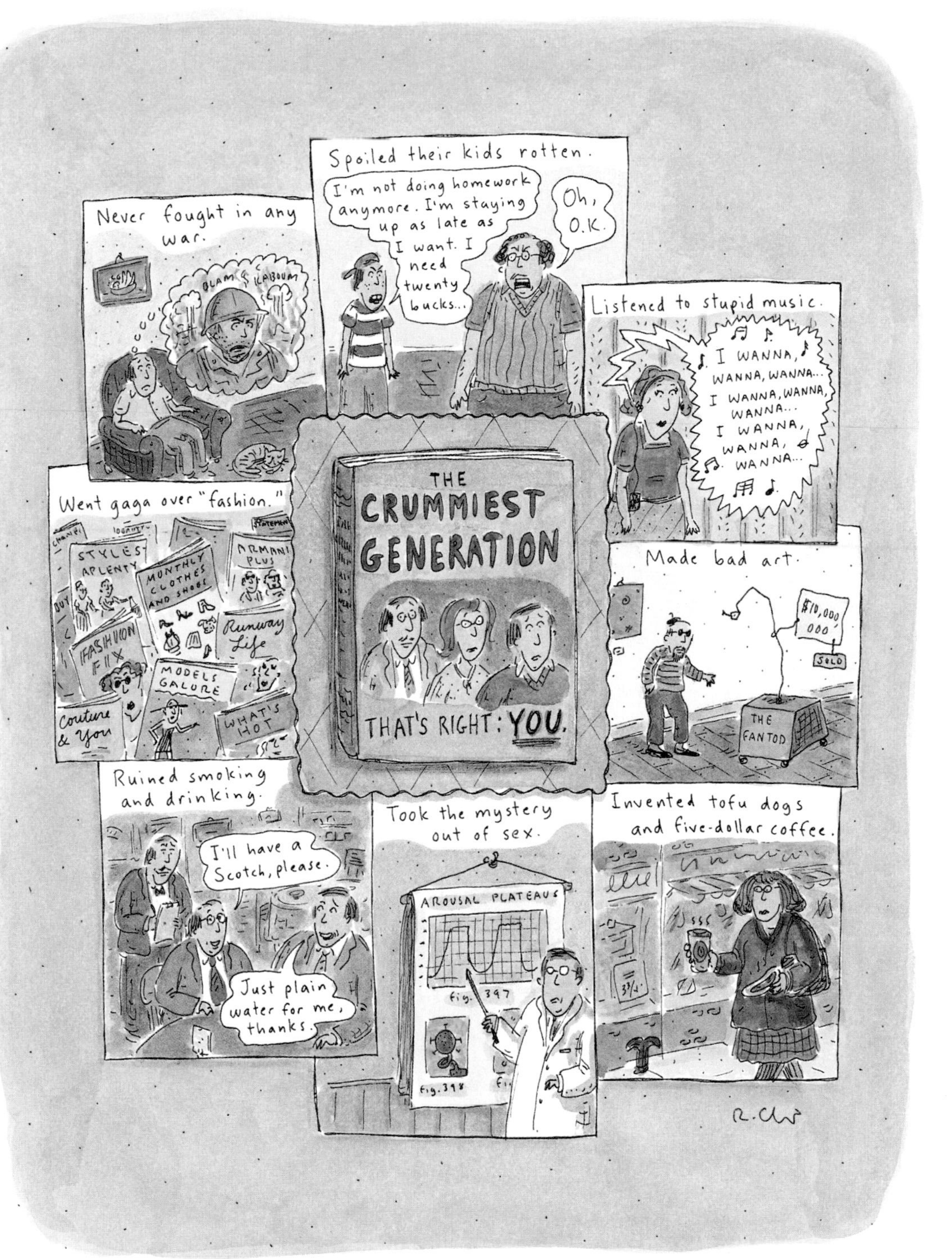
Never fought in any war.
BLAM
KABOUM
Spoiled their kids rotten.
I'm not doing homework anymore. I'm staying up as late as I want. I need twenty bucks...
Oh, O.K.
Listened to stupid music.
I WANNA, WANNA, WANNA... I WANNA, WANNA, WANNA... I WANNA, WANNA, WANNA...
Went gaga over "fashion."
STYLES APLENTY
MONTHLY CLOTHES AND SHOES
ARMANI PLUS
Runway Life
FASHION FIX
MODELS GALORE
WHAT'S HOT
Couture & You
THE CRUMMIEST GENERATION
THAT'S RIGHT: YOU.
Made bad art.
$10,000,000
SOLD
THE FANTOD
Ruined smoking and drinking.
I'll have a Scotch, please.
Just plain water for me, thanks.
Took the mystery out of sex.
AROUSAL PLATEAUS
fig. 397
fig. 398
Invented tofu dogs and five-dollar coffee.
R. Chast

BIRTH, BED, BATH, BEER,
BANKRUPTCY, BUNIONS, BIFOCALS,
BALDING, AND BEYOND.

THE NEW CAR

DRIVE
IDIOT
SORRY
MY MISTAKE
OOPS
WRONG
NEVER MIND
PARK
BREAK CAR
DECOY GEAR
STALL
UH-OH
THAT'S NOT IT
OUCH
SCARY SMELL
NEUTRAL
HYPERSPEED - I WISH
REVERSE

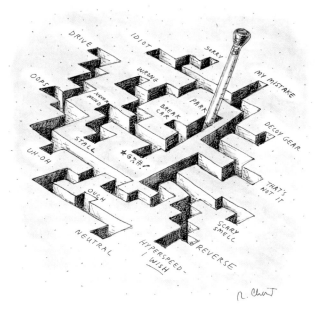

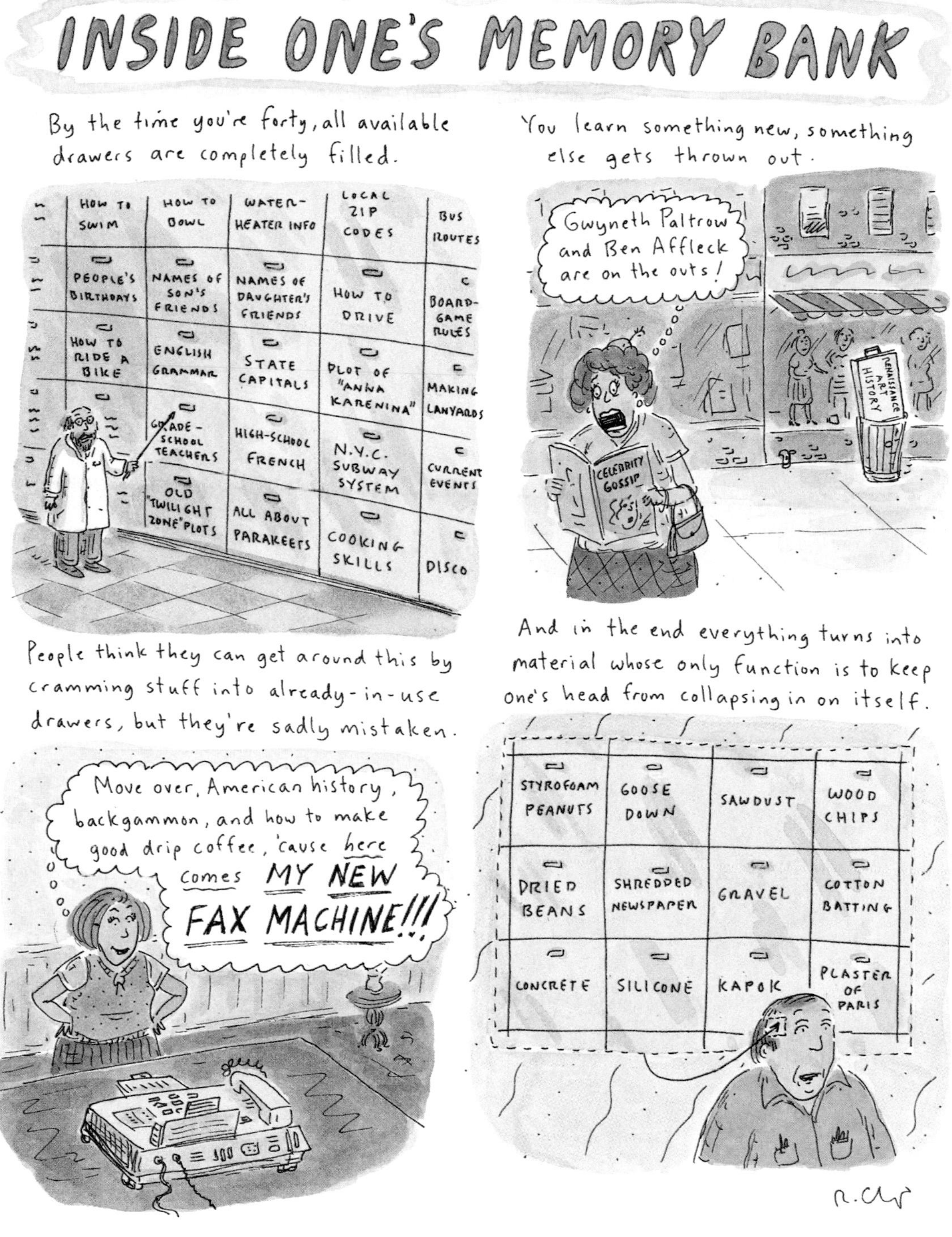
INSIDE ONE'S MEMORY BANK
By the time you're forty, all available drawers are completely filled.
HOW TO SWIM
HOW TO BOWL
WATER-HEATER INFO
LOCAL ZIP CODES
BUS ROUTES
PEOPLE'S BIRTHDAYS
NAMES OF SON'S FRIENDS
NAMES OF DAUGHTER'S FRIENDS
HOW TO DRIVE
BOARD-GAME RULES
HOW TO RIDE A BIKE
ENGLISH GRAMMAR
STATE CAPITALS
PLOT OF "ANNA KARENINA"
MAKING LANYARDS
GRADE-SCHOOL TEACHERS
HIGH-SCHOOL FRENCH
N.Y.C. SUBWAY SYSTEM
CURRENT EVENTS
OLD "TWILIGHT ZONE" PLOTS
ALL ABOUT PARAKEETS
COOKING SKILLS
DISCO
You learn something new, something else gets thrown out.
Gwyneth Paltrow and Ben Affleck are on the outs!
CELEBRITY GOSSIP
RENAISSANCE ART HISTORY
People think they can get around this by cramming stuff into already-in-use drawers, but they're sadly mistaken.
Move over, American history, backgammon, and how to make good drip coffee, 'cause here comes MY NEW FAX MACHINE!!!
And in the end everything turns into material whose only function is to keep one's head from collapsing in on itself.
STYROFOAM PEANUTS
GOOSE DOWN
SAWDUST
WOOD CHIPS
DRIED BEANS
SHREDDED NEWSPAPER
GRAVEL
COTTON BATTING
CONCRETE
SILICONE
KAPOK
PLASTER OF PARIS
R. Chast

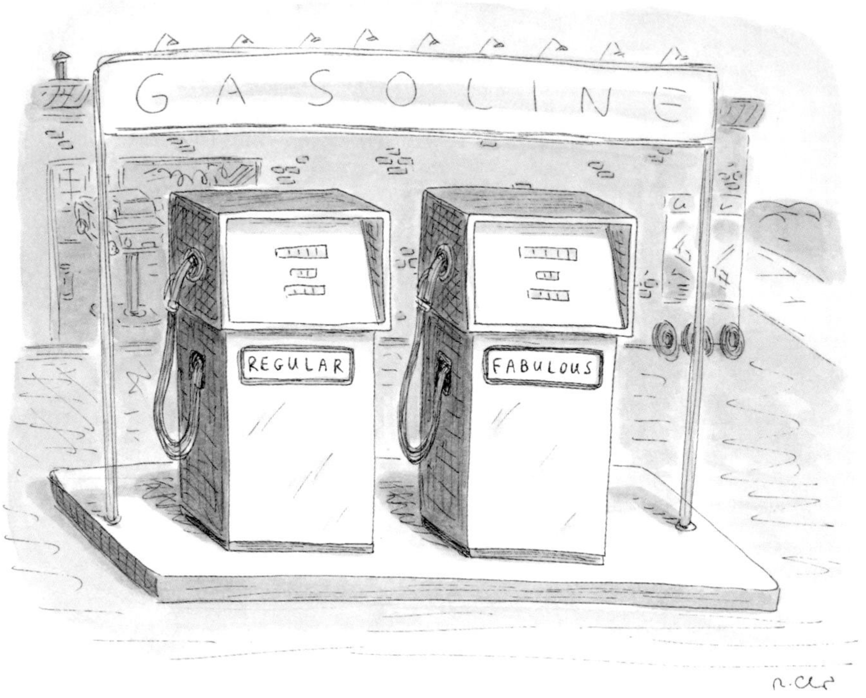
GASOLINE
REGULAR
FABULOUS

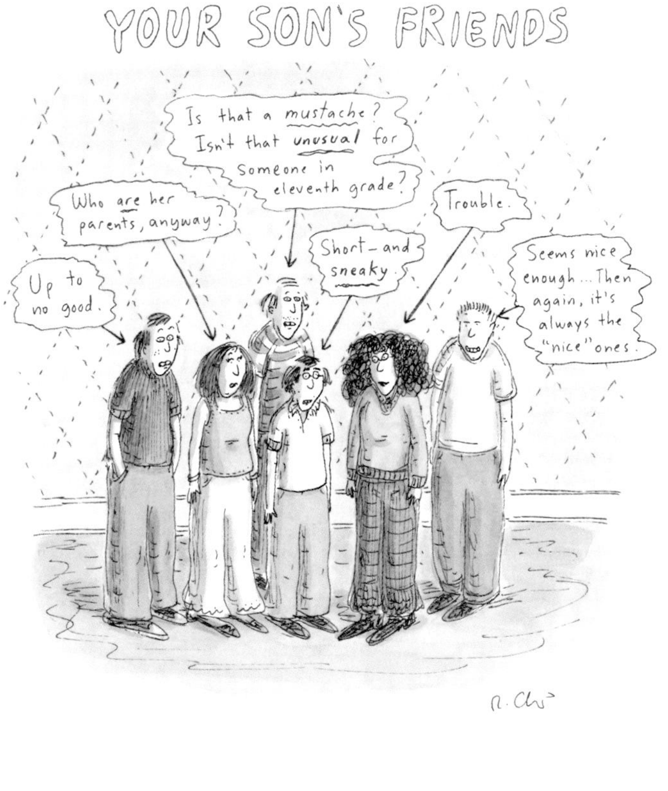
YOUR SON'S FRIENDS
Is that a mustache? Isn't that unusual for someone in eleventh grade?
Who are her parents, anyway?
Trouble.
Short—and sneaky.
Up to no good.
Seems nice enough... Then again, it's always the "nice" ones.

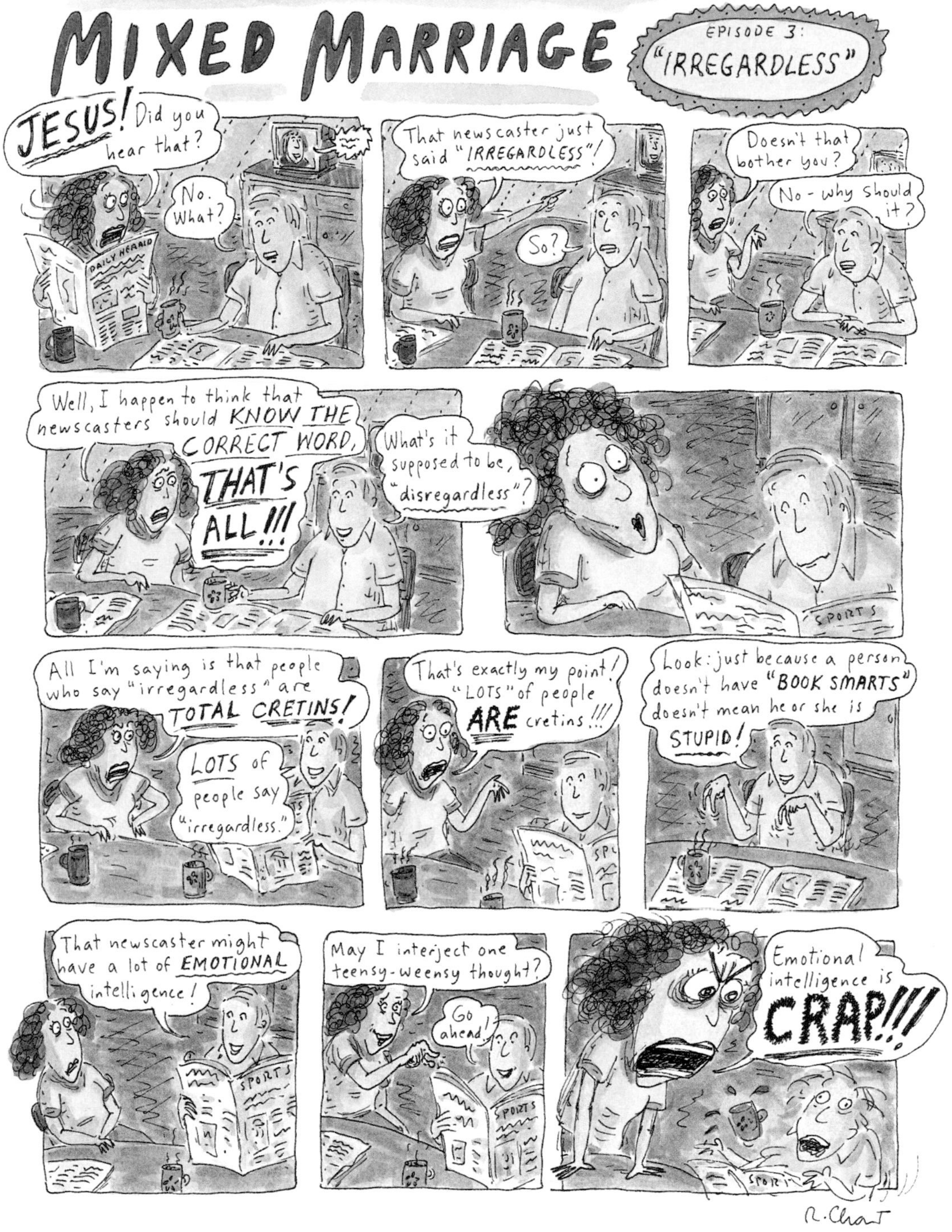
MIXED MARRIAGE
EPISODE 3: "IRREGARDLESS"
JESUS! Did you hear that?
No. What?
DAILY HERALD
That newscaster just said "IRREGARDLESS"!
So?
Doesn't that bother you?
No - why should it?
Well, I happen to think that newscasters should KNOW THE CORRECT WORD, THAT'S ALL!!!
What's it supposed to be, "disregardless"?
SPORTS
All I'm saying is that people who say "irregardless" are TOTAL CRETINS!
LOTS of people say "irregardless."
That's exactly my point! "LOTS" of people ARE cretins!!!
Look: just because a person doesn't have "BOOK SMARTS" doesn't mean he or she is STUPID!
That newscaster might have a lot of EMOTIONAL intelligence!
SPORTS
May I interject one teensy-weensy thought?
Go ahead!
SPORTS
Emotional intelligence is CRAP!!!
SPORTS
R. Chast

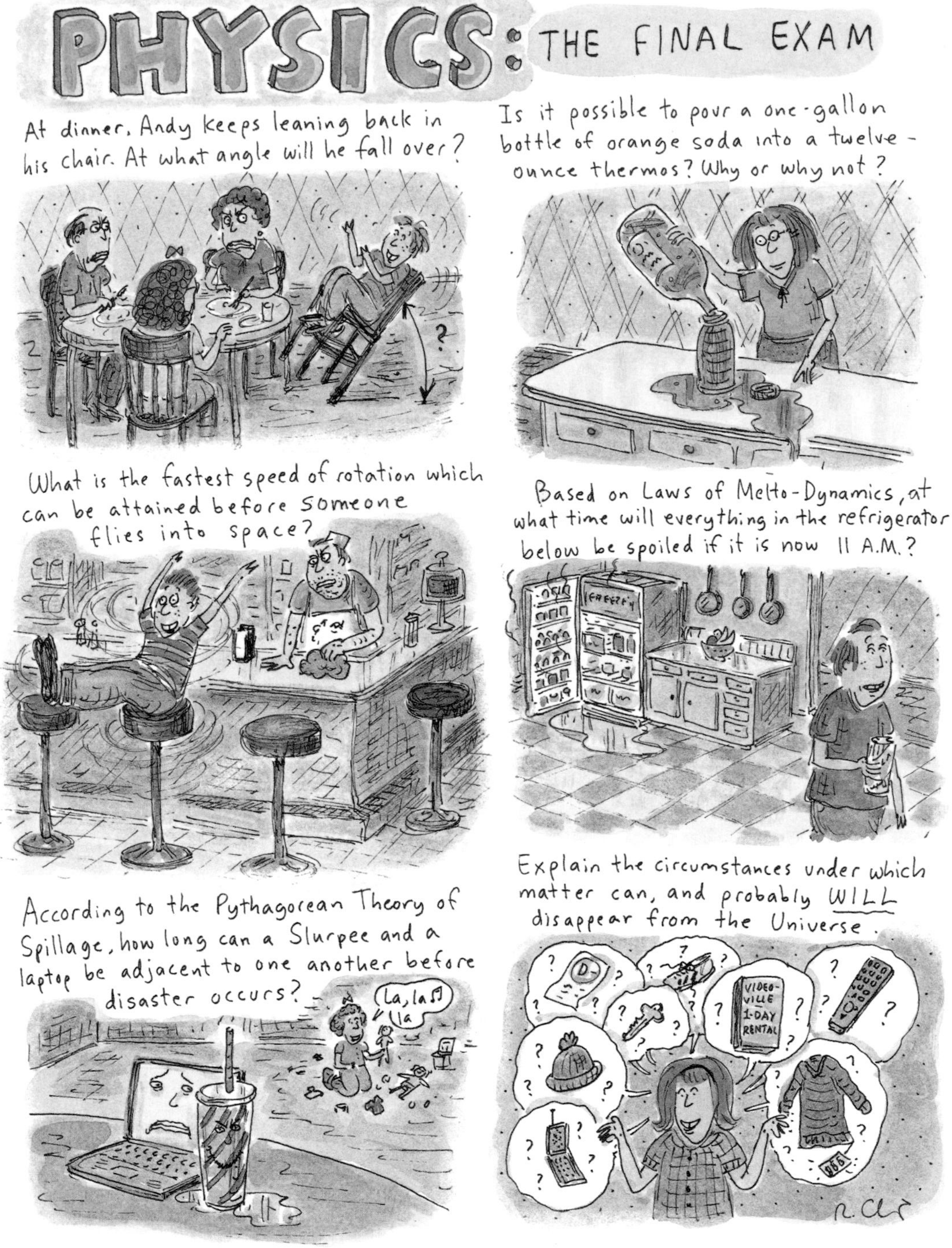
PHYSICS: THE FINAL EXAM
At dinner, Andy keeps leaning back in his chair. At what angle will he fall over?
?
Is it possible to pour a one-gallon bottle of orange soda into a twelve-ounce thermos? Why or why not?
What is the fastest speed of rotation which can be attained before someone flies into space?
Based on Laws of Melto-Dynamics, at what time will everything in the refrigerator below be spoiled if it is now 11 A.M.?
According to the Pythagorean Theory of Spillage, how long can a Slurpee and a laptop be adjacent to one another before disaster occurs?
La, la ♫ la
Explain the circumstances under which matter can, and probably WILL disappear from the Universe.
D-
VIDEO-VILLE 1-DAY RENTAL

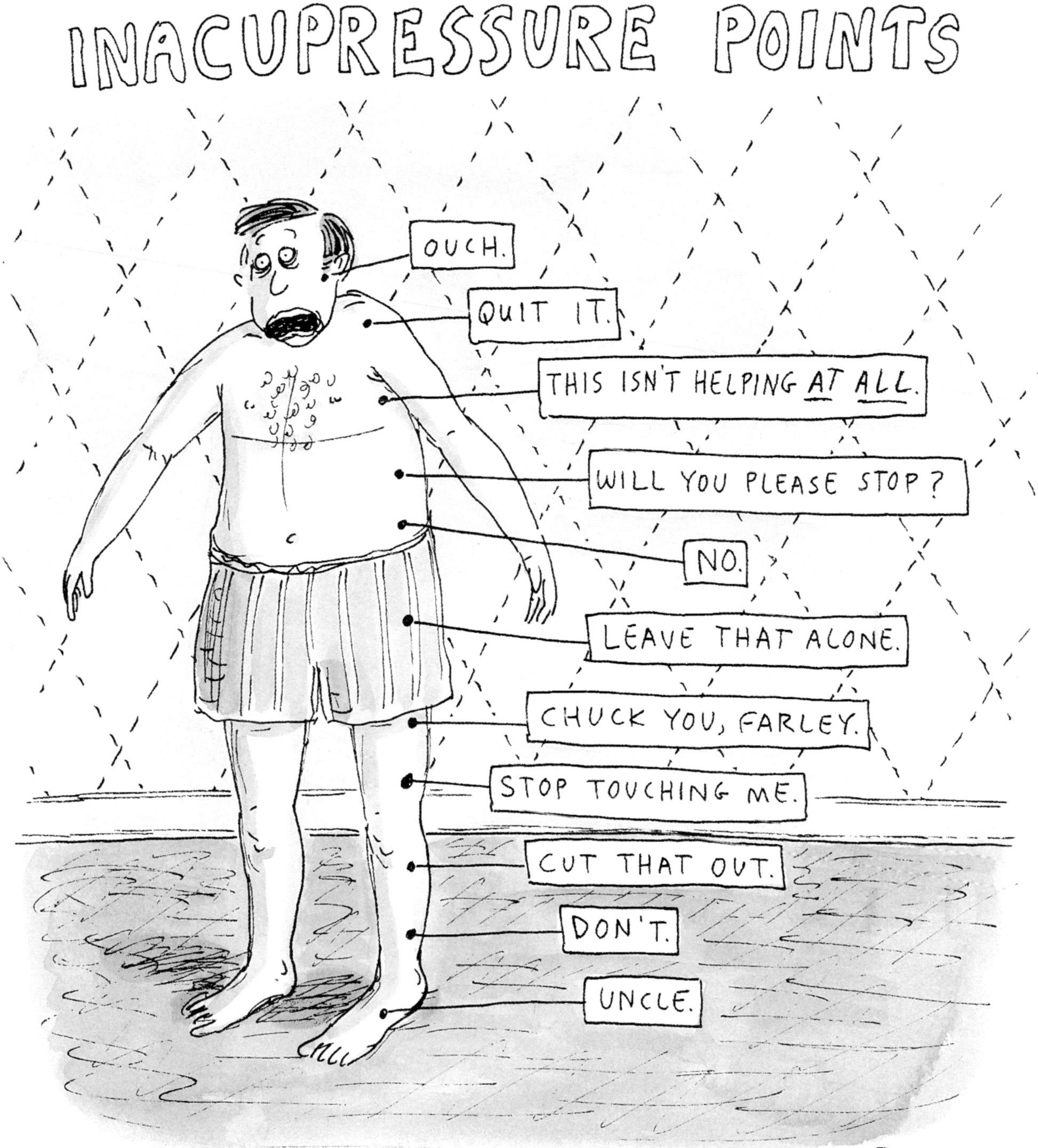
INACUPRESSURE POINTS
OUCH.
QUIT IT.
THIS ISN'T HELPING AT ALL.
WILL YOU PLEASE STOP?
NO.
LEAVE THAT ALONE.
CHUCK YOU, FARLEY.
STOP TOUCHING ME.
CUT THAT OUT.
DON'T.
UNCLE.

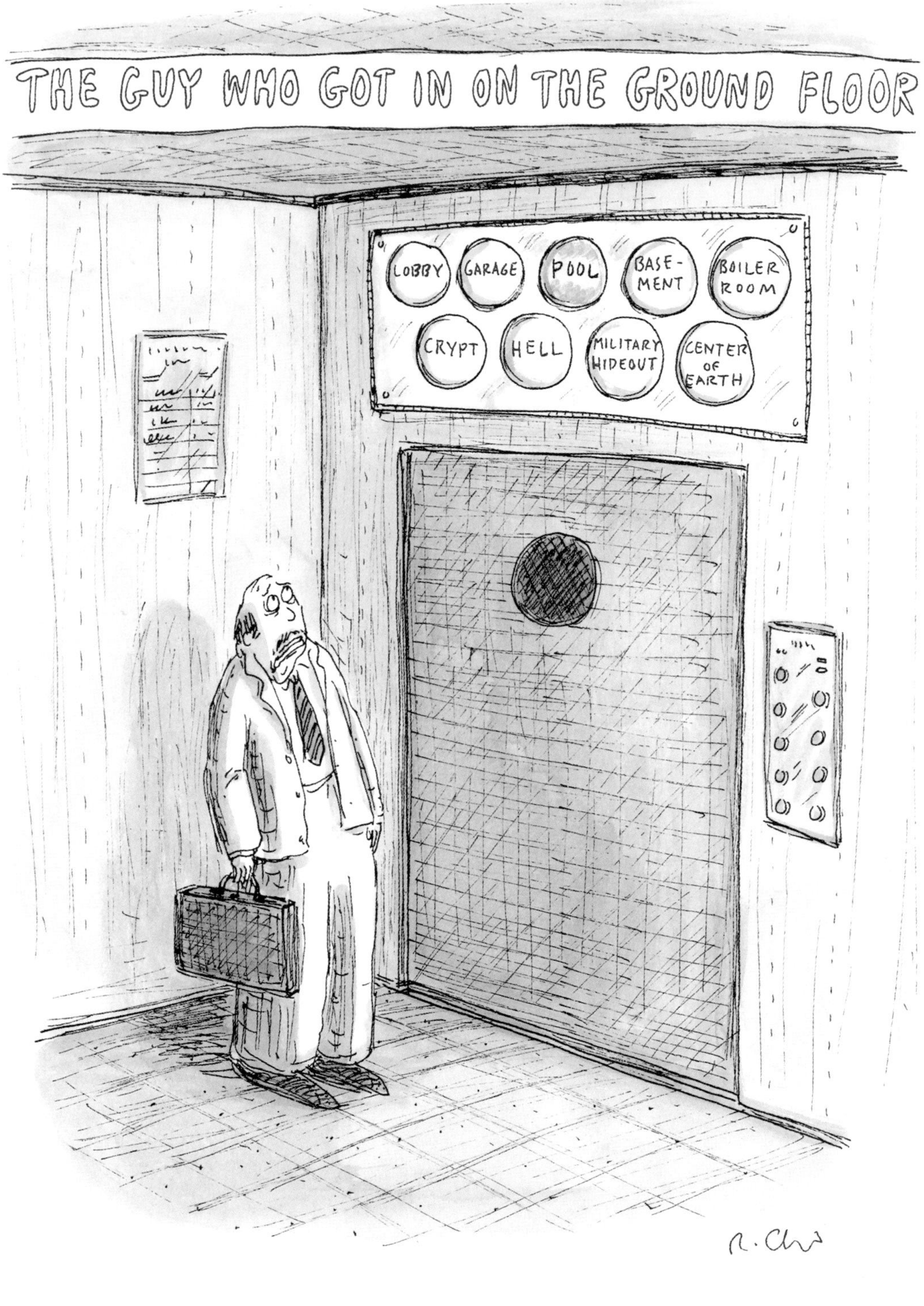
THE GUY WHO GOT IN ON THE GROUND FLOOR
LOBBY
GARAGE
POOL
BASE-MENT
BOILER ROOM
CRYPT
HELL
MILITARY HIDEOUT
CENTER OF EARTH

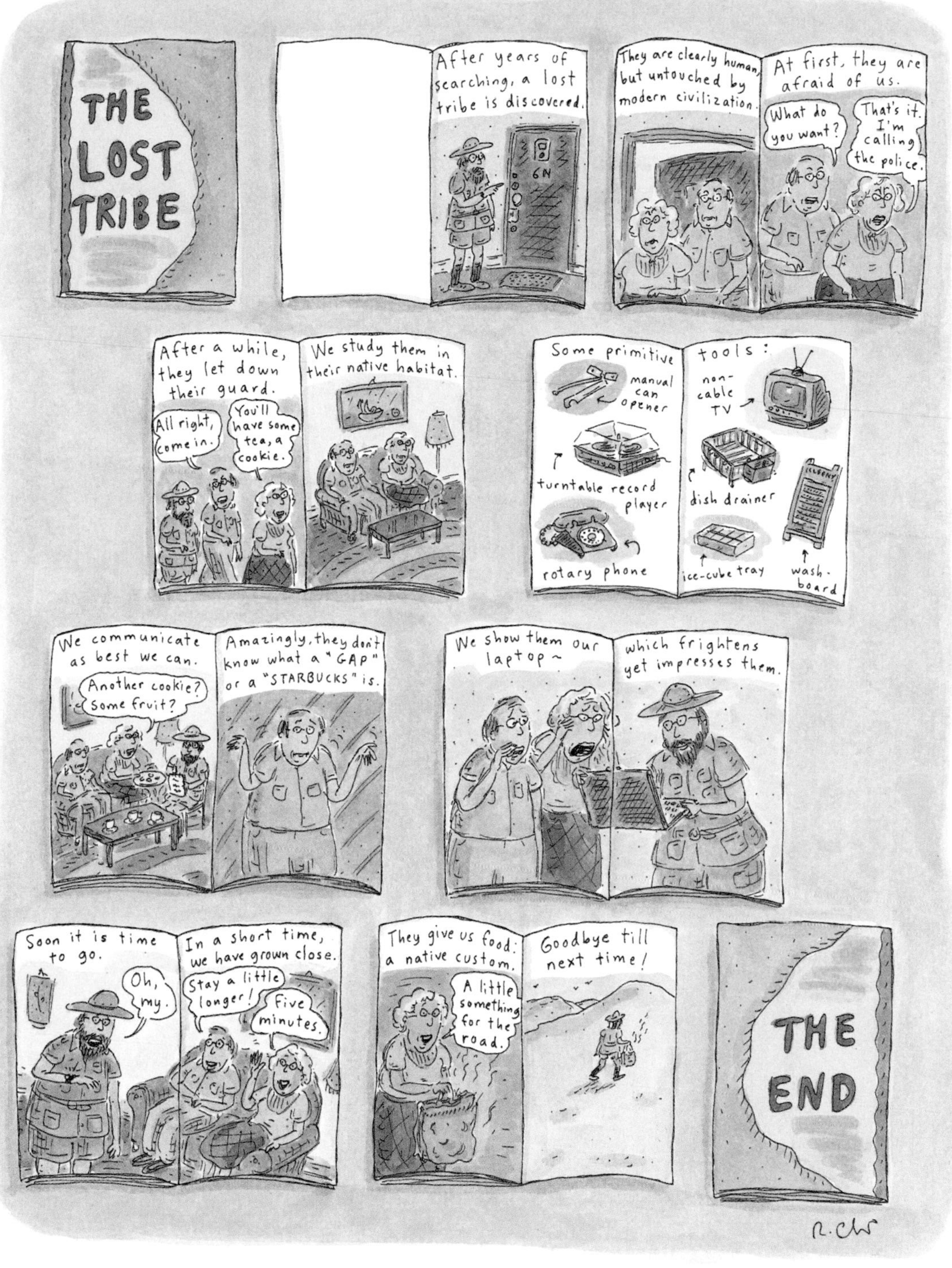
THE LOST TRIBE
After years of searching, a lost tribe is discovered.
6N
They are clearly human, but untouched by modern civilization.
At first, they are afraid of us.
What do you want?
That's it. I'm calling the police.
After a while, they let down their guard.
All right, come in.
You'll have some tea, a cookie.
We study them in their native habitat.
Some primitive tools:
manual can opener
turntable record player
rotary phone
non-cable TV
dish drainer
ice-cube tray
wash-board
We communicate as best we can.
Another cookie? Some fruit?
Amazingly, they don't know what a "GAP" or a "STARBUCKS" is.
We show them our laptop ~
which frightens yet impresses them.
Soon it is time to go.
Oh, my.
In a short time, we have grown close.
Stay a little longer!
Five minutes.
They give us food: a native custom.
A little something for the road.
Goodbye till next time!
THE END
R. Chst

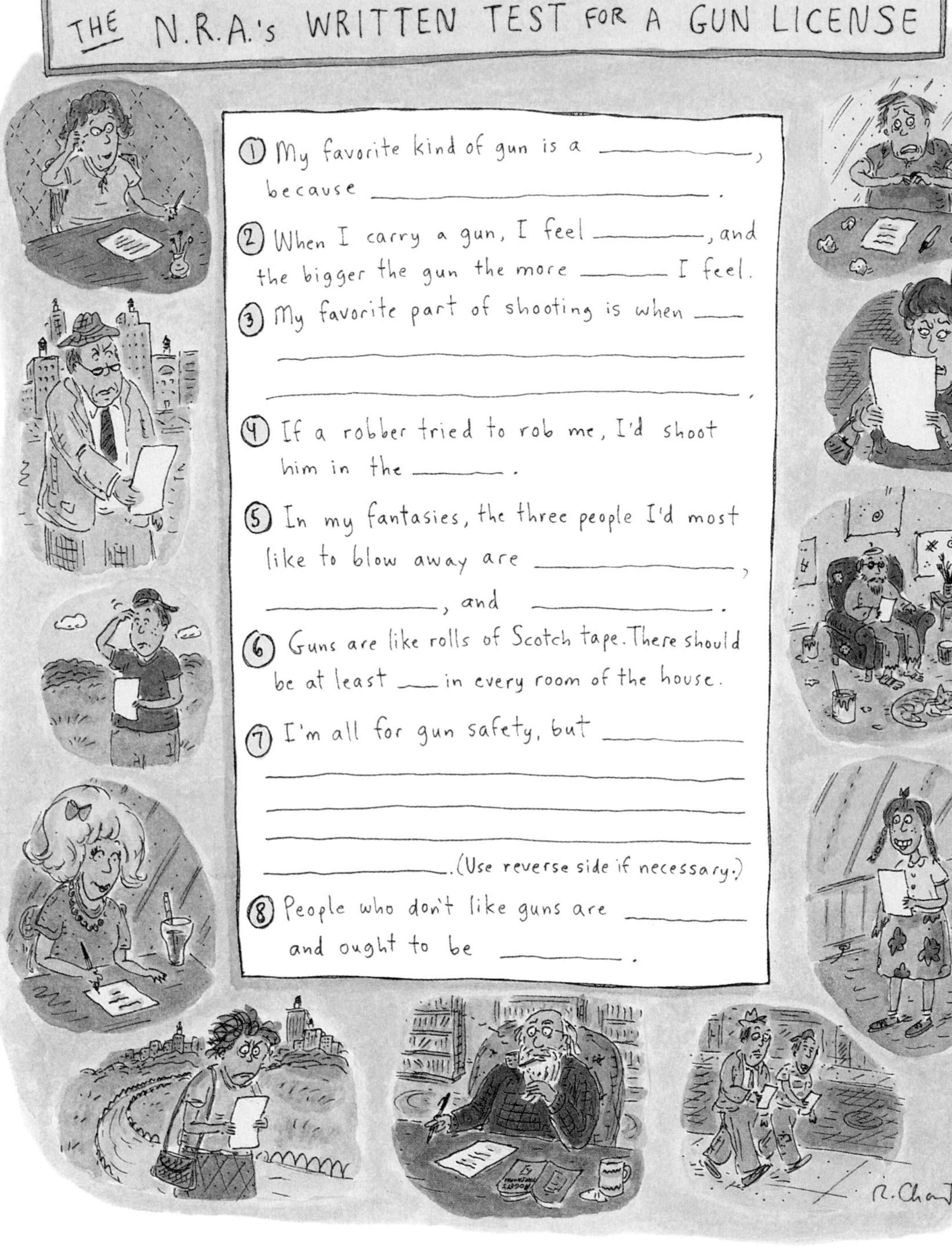
THE N.R.A.'s WRITTEN TEST FOR A GUN LICENSE
1 My favorite kind of gun is a ________, because ________.
2 When I carry a gun, I feel ________, and the bigger the gun the more ______ I feel.
3 My favorite part of shooting is when ________.
4 If a robber tried to rob me, I'd shoot him in the ______.
5 In my fantasies, the three people I'd most like to blow away are ________, ________, and ________.
6 Guns are like rolls of Scotch tape. There should be at least ___ in every room of the house.
7 I'm all for gun safety, but ________. (Use reverse side if necessary.)
8 People who don't like guns are ______ and ought to be ______.
R. Chast

GRAIN OF SAND
BACK
RELOAD
FORWARD
???? HELP
STOP
Address
http://www.grainofsand.com
WELCOME TO THE
Universe in a Grain of Sand
PAGE
YOU ARE VISITOR 000000000001
LINKS:
MY BEST FRIENDS (LAST UPDATED 11/99)
FOODS I LIKE, FOODS I HATE
COURTNEY'S HOME PAGE
STUFFED ANIMALS
MY DRAWINGS OF HORSES
POKEMON
MY ABSURD 'RENTS
SCULPTURE
AUSTRALIA
BRUCE SPRINGSTEEN
VINNIE'S VACATION LINKS
THE JERSEY SHORE
NASSAU
PLACES AUNT FRIEDA HAS NEVER BEEN AND SWEARS SHE'LL NEVER GO
COUNTRY FAIRS
COUNTRY FAIR SOUVENIRS
SPIN ART
COLORED SAND LAYERED IN BOTTLES
FRIED DOUGH
Hey, Jethro.
WHERE HILLBILLIES GO FOR FUN
THE HILLBILLY HOME PAGE
THE PICA PAGE
DIRT
SAND
OZARKS
WHERE HILLBILLIES LIVE
Al, we're not so bad!
THE WIDE WORLD OF SAND CRAFTS
SAND PAINTINGS
SAND: TO EAT OR NOT TO EAT?
MAINSTAY OF BEACHES
CERAMICS
ART: WHAT IS IT?
SAND CASTLES
MY AWFUL RELATIVES
MY AWFUL JOB
AL'S HOME PAGE
SAND: WHAT IS IT?
It's one-of-a-kind.
UGLY MUGS
SAND CANDLE LINKS
SAND IN EAR
SAND IN PANTS
DATE PALMS
A DESERT STAPLE
CAMELS
PYRAMIDS
SAND IN TEETH
SAND-RELATED INJURIES
THINGS HIPPIES MADE
DISEASES, WAIST UP
DIRTY ROY'S FETISH PAGE
ELEPHANTIASIS
Heh, heh.
CHEESE
THOSE WEIRD BELTS THAT LOOK LIKE THEY'RE MADE IN GUATEMALA BUT AREN'T
SOURCES OF LIGHT FROM A TO Z
CRUNCH
SAND IN EYE
LOCKJAW
DISEASES WAIST DOWN
SAND IN SHOE
LAMPS
THE UNIVERSE: WHAT IS IT?
EYE AILMENTS
THE BIG PAGE OF DISEASES
YOU DON'T WANT TO KNOW
CRUNCH, CRUNCH
TONS OF STARS
HYPOCHONDRIA CHAT
OUR SUN
THREE OR FOUR PLANETS, TOPS
RARE AND TERRIBLE DISEASES
ELECTRICAL APPLIANCES
HUGE, EMPTY GASEOUS AREAS IN SPACE
HOW DO YOU KNOW I DON'T HAVE THE BUBONIC PLAGUE?
HEIGHTS
FREE MONEY (AS IF)
I KNOW I GREW IN YOUR TUMMY, BUT HOW DID I GET IN YOUR TUMMY?
THE ANXIETY SITE
WHAT'S THAT BIG WART ON YOUR FACE?
ANNOYING QUESTIONS ASKED BY CHILDREN
HOW MUCH MONEY DO YOU MAKE?
ALL ABOUT MONEY
WHERE'S MY BIKE HELMET?
SEX AND ALL ABOUT IT

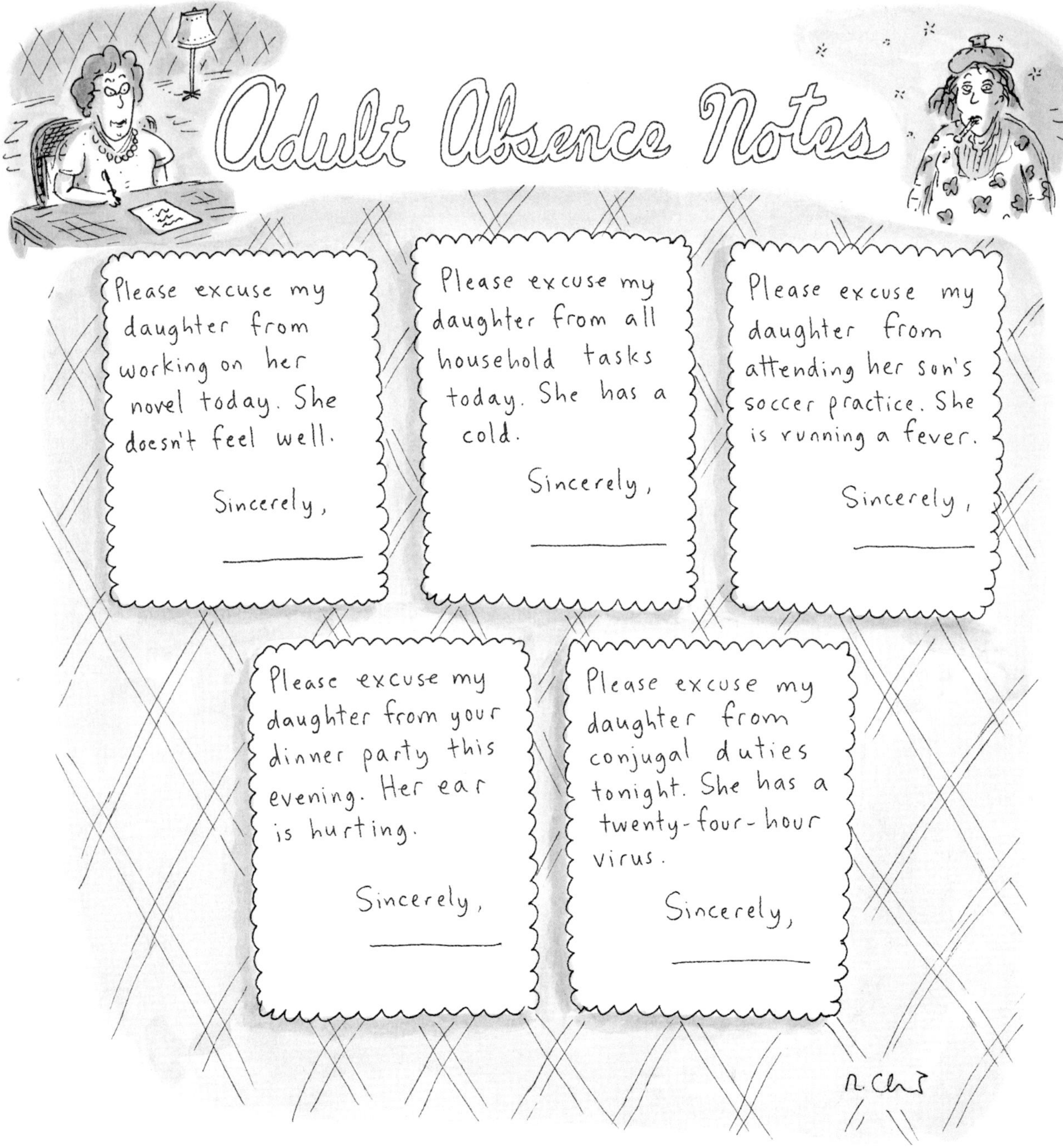
Adult Absence Notes
Please excuse my daughter from working on her novel today. She doesn't feel well. Sincerely,
Please excuse my daughter from all household tasks today. She has a cold. Sincerely,
Please excuse my daughter from attending her son's soccer practice. She is running a fever. Sincerely,
Please excuse my daughter from your dinner party this evening. Her ear is hurting. Sincerely,
Please excuse my daughter from conjugal duties tonight. She has a twenty-four-hour virus. Sincerely,

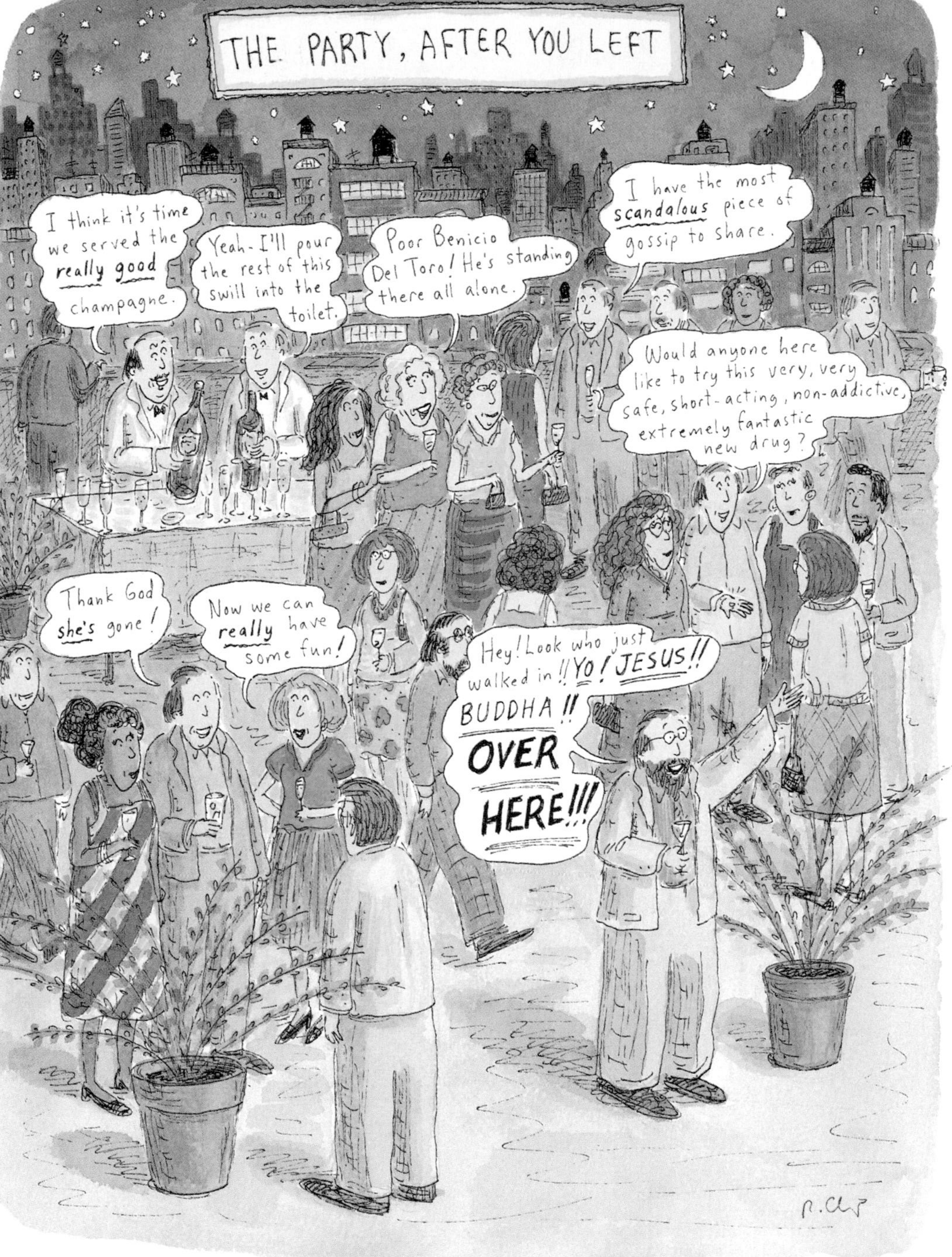
THE PARTY, AFTER YOU LEFT
I think it's time we served the really good champagne.
Yeah - I'll pour the rest of this swill into the toilet.
Poor Benicio Del Toro! He's standing there all alone.
I have the most scandalous piece of gossip to share.
Would anyone here like to try this very, very safe, short-acting, non-addictive, extremely fantastic new drug?
Thank God she's gone!
Now we can really have some fun!
Hey! Look who just walked in!! YO! JESUS!! BUDDHA!! OVER HERE!!!

I HATE YOU! You're RUINING MY LIFE!!!
Look! It's right here on page 4,283!
THE BIG BOOK OF PARENT-CHILD FIGHTS
I want to see every last bite of that broccoli GONE.
TABLE OF CONTENTS
1. Food Arguments .... page 1
2. Bedtime Feuds 832
3. Personal-Hygiene Tiffs 1,247
4. School-Related Spats 1,960
5. Allowance Rhubarbs 2,847
6. Clothing Squabbles 3,563
7. Choice of Friends Scraps 3,999
8. Chore Disputes 5,048
9. Messy-Room Run-Ins 5,876
10. Sibling-Associated Skirmishes 7,114
11. General-Ingratitude Quarrels 7,892
12. Miscellaneous Battles 9,505
I'm quitting piano.
You made a commitment, and you're going to stick to it, young lady.
But Allison gets to stay up till 3 A.M. on school nights!
???
You don't appreciate anything! You just sit there and TAKE IT ALL FOR GRANTED!!!
Go take a shower.
Make me.
She touched my stuff.
Did not.
Did too.
Liar.
Stop it! Stop it!! Stopitstopitstopit stopitstopit!!!
A C+ in English? What is the meaning of this???
Ma, everybody's wearing pants like these.
Look. Just because Jamie has a shaved head and her dad is in jail and her mom is a stripper and her brother supposedly deals drugs and her sister has three kids out of wedlock is no reason to...
Mom, I can't find my phone.
Walk the damn dog. NOW.
But I'm downloading something.
But Allison gets ten dollars a week!

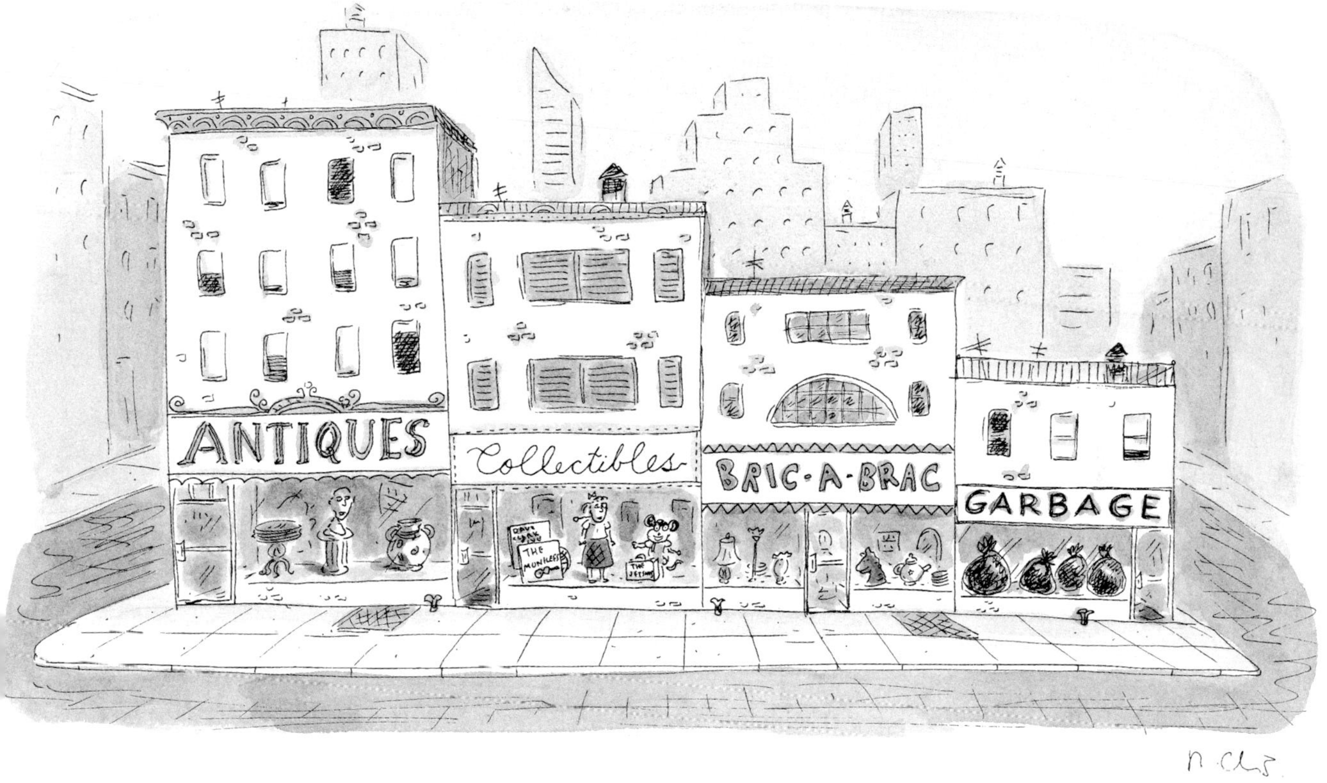
ANTIQUES
Collectibles
BRIC-A-BRAC
GARBAGE

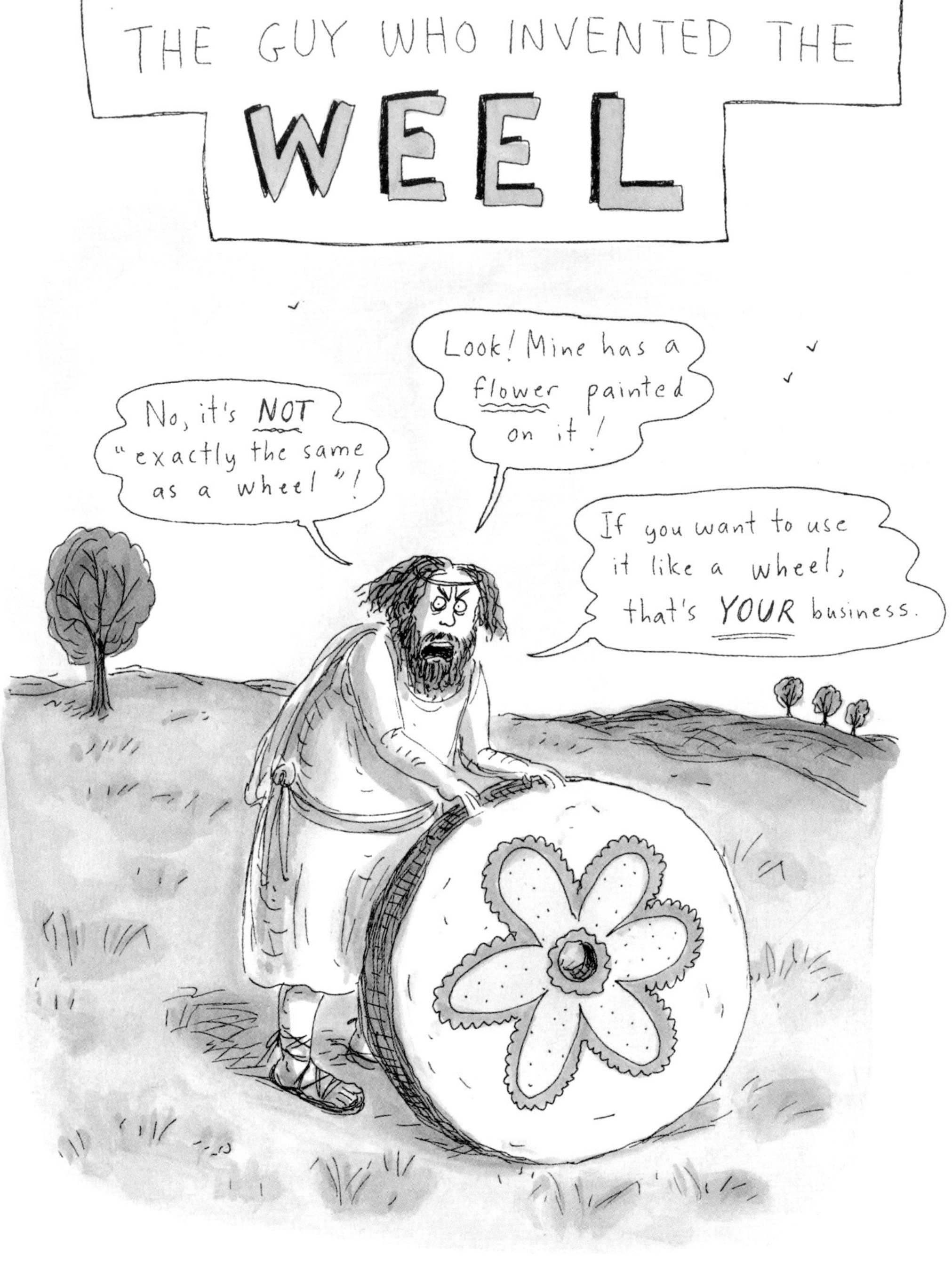
THE GUY WHO INVENTED THE
WEEL
No, it's NOT "exactly the same as a wheel"!
Look! Mine has a flower painted on it!
If you want to use it like a wheel, that's YOUR business.
R. Chast

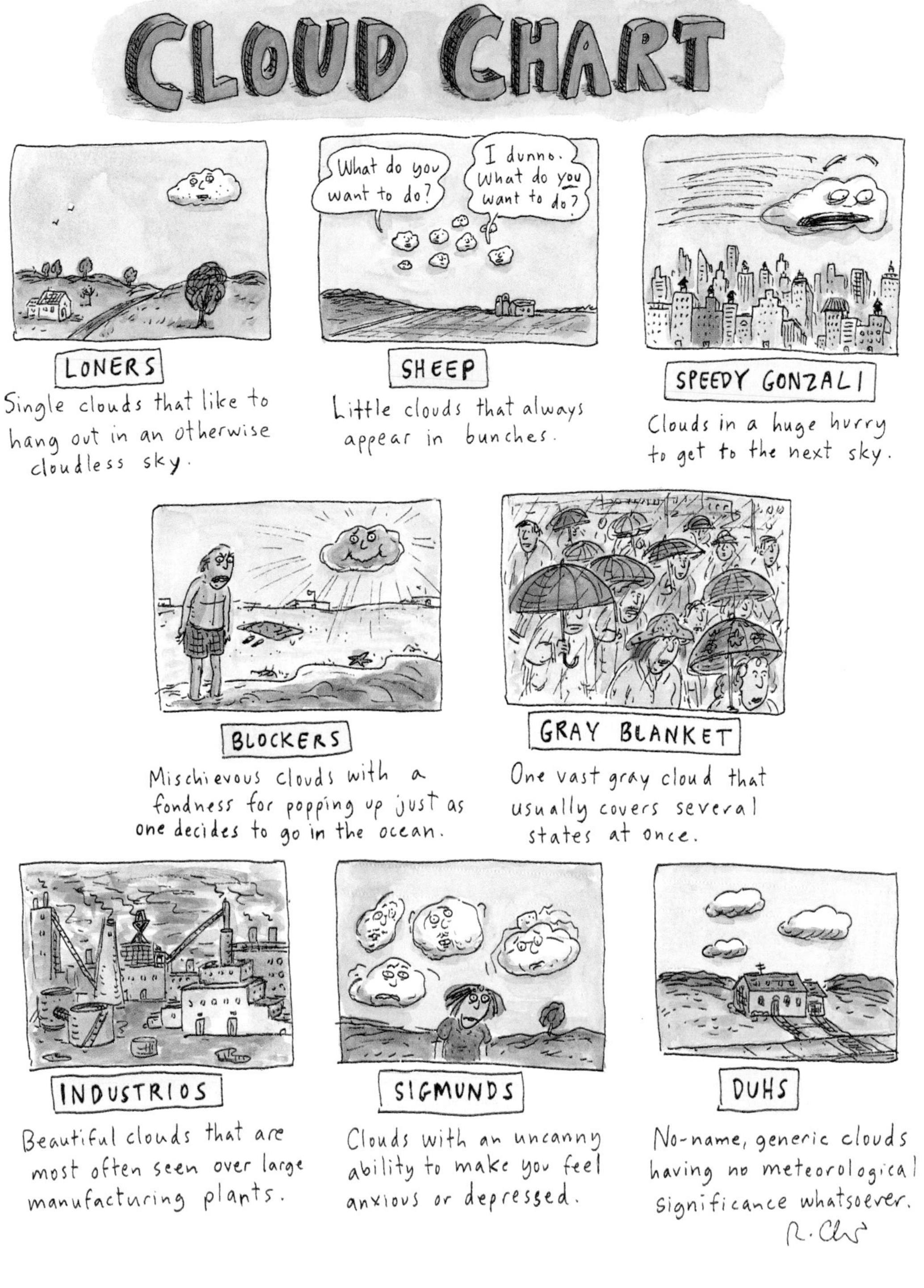
CLOUD CHART
LONERS
Single clouds that like to hang out in an otherwise cloudless sky.
What do you want to do?
I dunno. What do you want to do?
SHEEP
Little clouds that always appear in bunches.
SPEEDY GONZALI
Clouds in a huge hurry to get to the next sky.
BLOCKERS
Mischievous clouds with a fondness for popping up just as one decides to go in the ocean.
GRAY BLANKET
One vast gray cloud that usually covers several states at once.
INDUSTRIOS
Beautiful clouds that are most often seen over large manufacturing plants.
SIGMUNDS
Clouds with an uncanny ability to make you feel anxious or depressed.
DUHS
No-name, generic clouds having no meteorological significance whatsoever.
R. Chr

DOG DAY

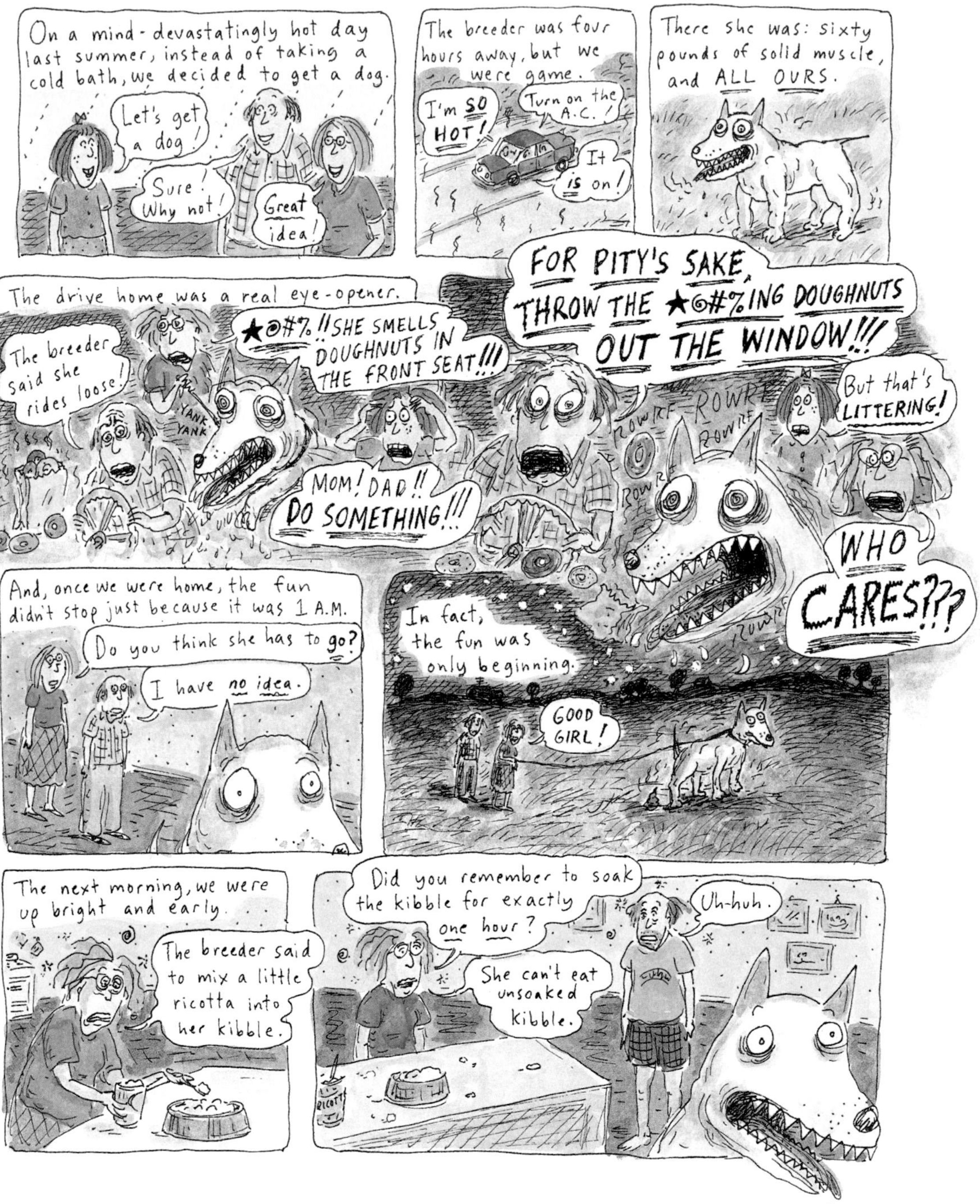
On a mind-devastatingly hot day last summer, instead of taking a cold bath, we decided to get a dog.
Let's get a dog!
Sure! Why not!
Great idea!
The breeder was four hours away, but we were game.
I'm SO HOT!
Turn on the A.C.!
It is on!
There she was: sixty pounds of solid muscle, and ALL OURS.
The drive home was a real eye-opener.
The breeder said she rides loose!
YANK YANK
★@#%!! SHE SMELLS DOUGHNUTS IN THE FRONT SEAT!!!
MOM! DAD!! DO SOMETHING!!!
FOR PITY'S SAKE, THROW THE ★@#%ING DOUGHNUTS OUT THE WINDOW!!!
ROWRF ROWRF ROWRF
But that's LITTERING!
WHO CARES???
And, once we were home, the fun didn't stop just because it was 1 A.M.
Do you think she has to go?
I have no idea.
In fact, the fun was only beginning.
GOOD GIRL!
The next morning, we were up bright and early.
The breeder said to mix a little ricotta into her kibble.
Did you remember to soak the kibble for exactly one hour?
Uh-huh.
She can't eat unsoaked kibble.

AFTERNOON

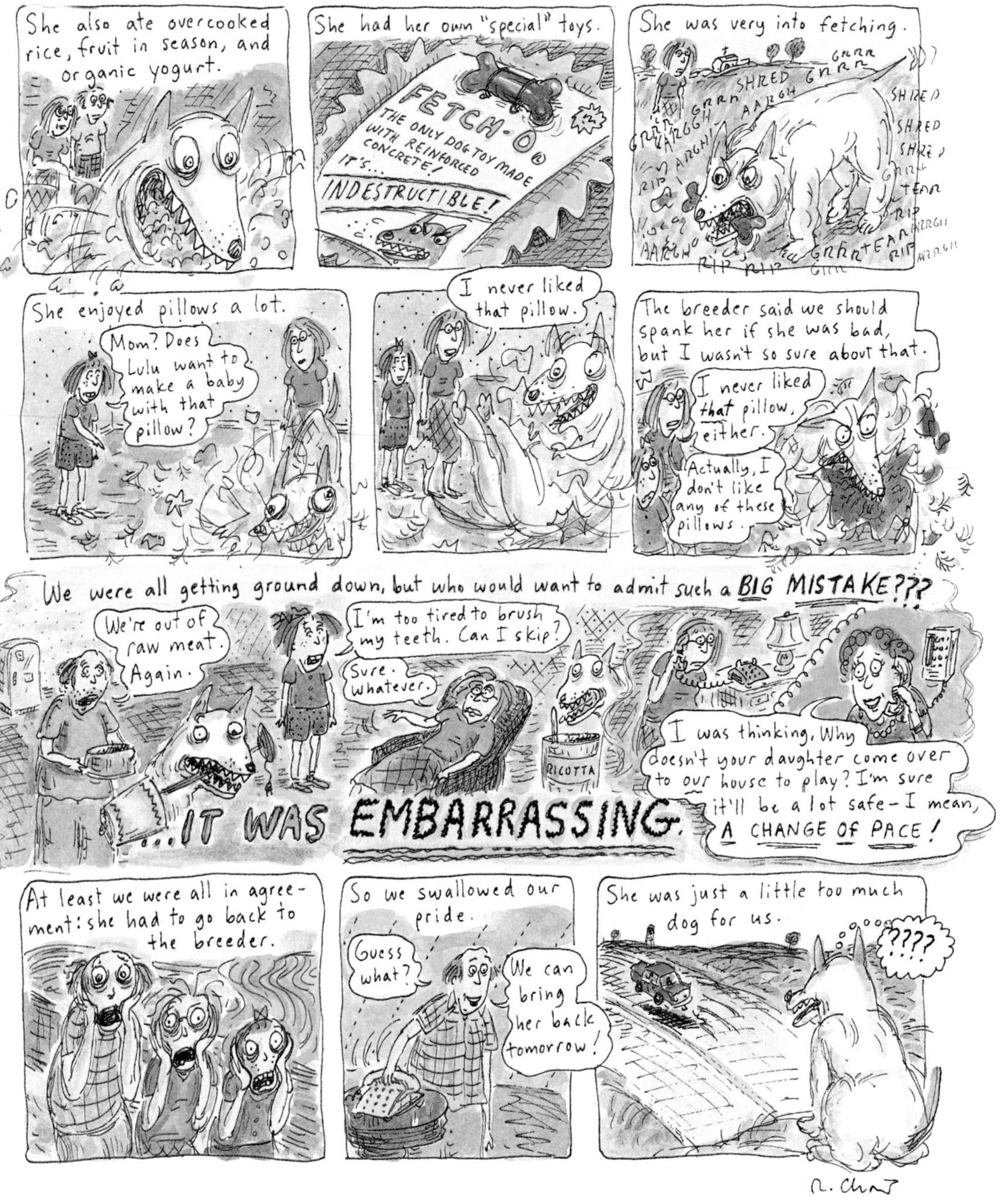

She also ate overcooked rice, fruit in season, and organic yogurt.
She had her own "special" toys.
FETCH-O® THE ONLY DOG TOY MADE WITH REINFORCED CONCRETE! IT'S... INDESTRUCTIBLE!
She was very into fetching.
GRRR SHRED GRRR AARGH RIP SHRED SHRED TEAR RIP TEAR AARGH RIP
She enjoyed pillows a lot.
Mom? Does Lulu want to make a baby with that pillow?
I never liked that pillow.
The breeder said we should spank her if she was bad, but I wasn't so sure about that.
I never liked that pillow, either.
Actually, I don't like any of these pillows.
We were all getting ground down, but who would want to admit such a BIG MISTAKE???
We're out of raw meat. Again.
I'm too tired to brush my teeth. Can I skip?
Sure. whatever.
RICOTTA
I was thinking, Why doesn't your daughter come over to our house to play? I'm sure it'll be a lot safe– I mean, A CHANGE OF PACE!
...IT WAS EMBARRASSING.
At least we were all in agreement: she had to go back to the breeder.
So we swallowed our pride.
Guess what?
We can bring her back tomorrow!
She was just a little too much dog for us.
????
R. Chast

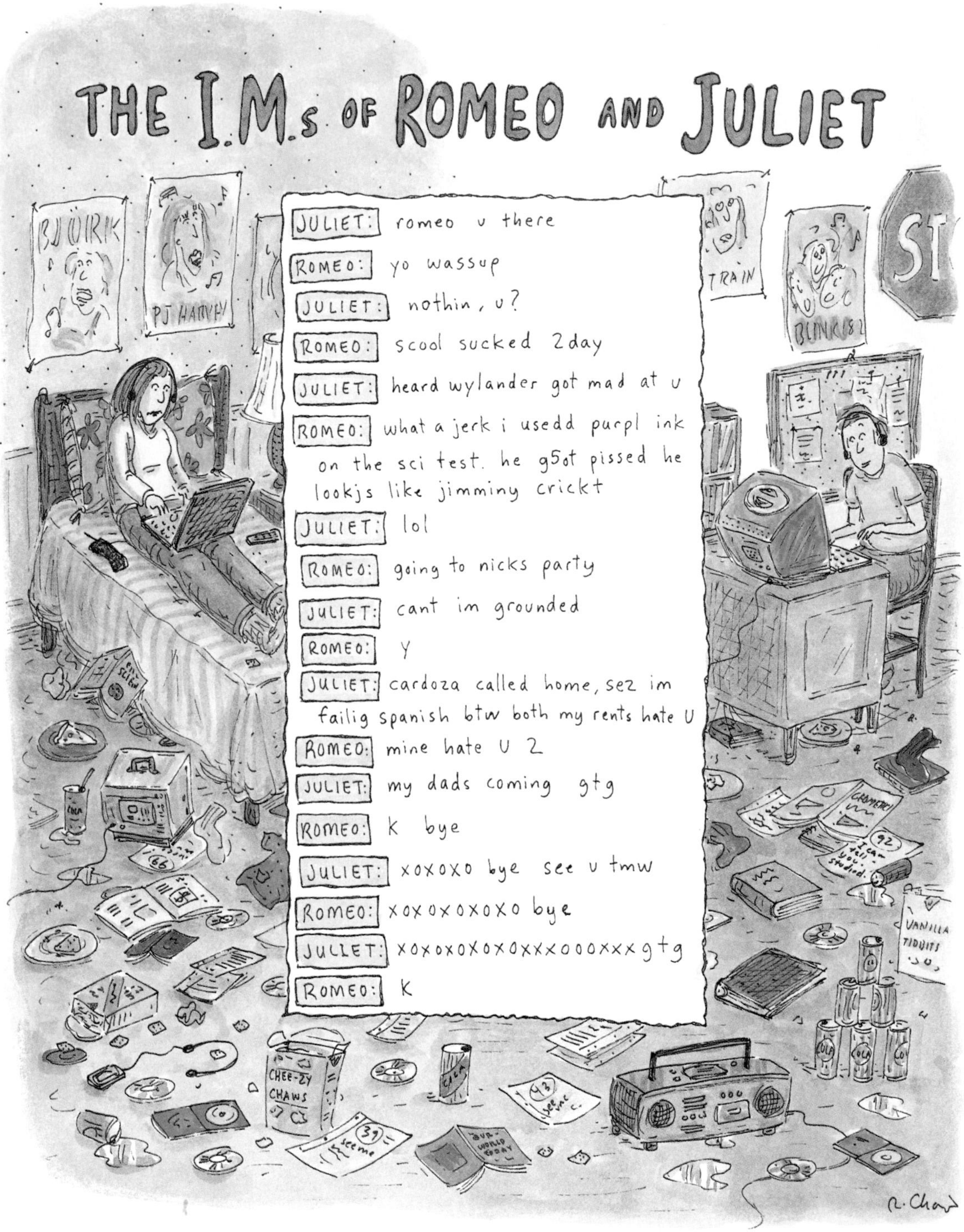
THE I.M.s OF ROMEO AND JULIET
JULIET: romeo u there
ROMEO: yo wassup
JULIET: nothin, u?
ROMEO: scool sucked 2day
JULIET: heard wylander got mad at u
ROMEO: what a jerk i usedd purpl ink on the sci test. he g5ot pissed he lookjs like jimminy crickt
JULIET: lol
ROMEO: going to nicks party
JULIET: cant im grounded
ROMEO: Y
JULIET: cardoza called home, sez im failig spanish btw both my rents hate U
ROMEO: mine hate U 2
JULIET: my dads coming gtg
ROMEO: K bye
JULIET: xoxoxo bye see u tmw
ROMEO: xoxoxoxoxo bye
JULIET: xoxoxoxoxoxxxoooxxxgtg
ROMEO: K
BJORK
PJ HARVEY
TRAIN
BLINK 182
CHEE-ZY CHAWS
VANILLA TIDBITS
see me
R. Chast

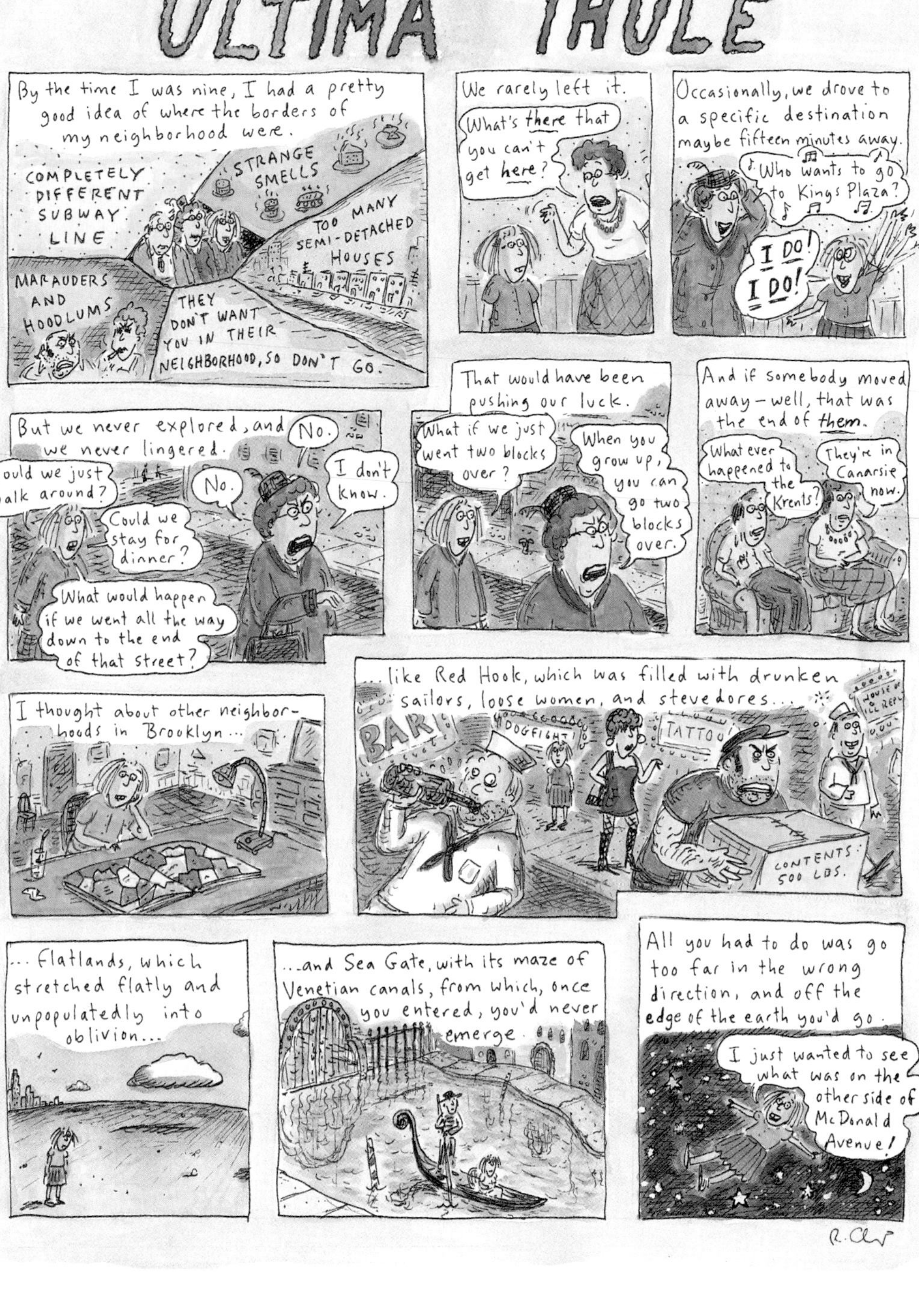
ULTIMA THULE
By the time I was nine, I had a pretty good idea of where the borders of my neighborhood were.
COMPLETELY DIFFERENT SUBWAY LINE
STRANGE SMELLS
TOO MANY SEMI-DETACHED HOUSES
MARAUDERS AND HOODLUMS
THEY DON'T WANT YOU IN THEIR NEIGHBORHOOD, SO DON'T GO.
We rarely left it.
What's there that you can't get here?
Occasionally, we drove to a specific destination maybe fifteen minutes away.
Who wants to go to Kings Plaza?
I DO! I DO!
But we never explored, and we never lingered.
Could we just walk around?
No.
Could we stay for dinner?
No.
What would happen if we went all the way down to the end of that street?
I don't know.
That would have been pushing our luck.
What if we just went two blocks over?
When you grow up, you can go two blocks over.
And if somebody moved away—well, that was the end of them.
Whatever happened to the Krents?
They're in Canarsie now.
I thought about other neighborhoods in Brooklyn...
...like Red Hook, which was filled with drunken sailors, loose women, and stevedores...
BAR
DOGFIGHT
TATTOO
CONTENTS 500 LBS.
...Flatlands, which stretched flatly and unpopulatedly into oblivion...
...and Sea Gate, with its maze of Venetian canals, from which, once you entered, you'd never emerge.
All you had to do was go too far in the wrong direction, and off the edge of the earth you'd go.
I just wanted to see what was on the other side of McDonald Avenue!
R. Chast

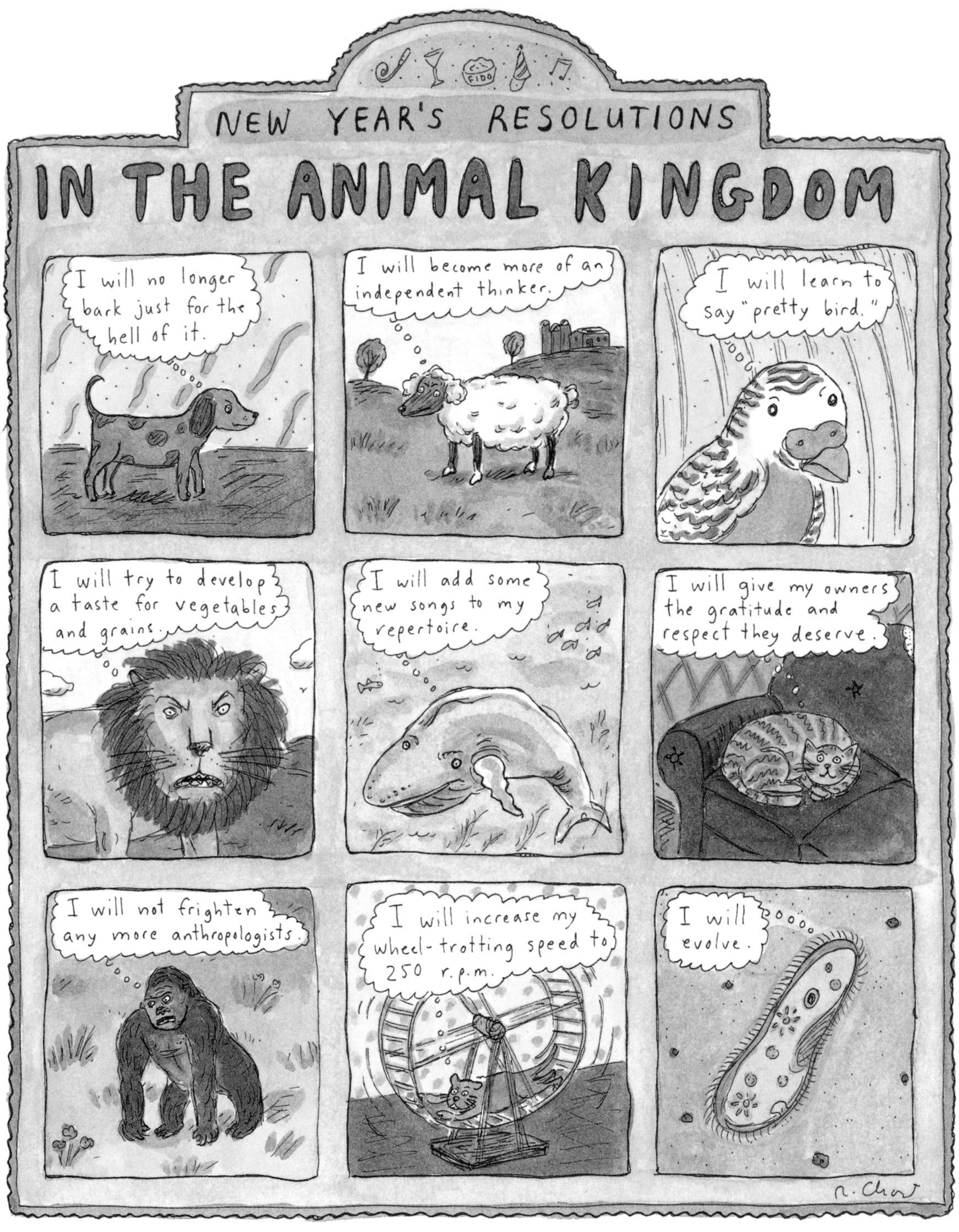
FIDO
NEW YEAR'S RESOLUTIONS
IN THE ANIMAL KINGDOM
I will no longer bark just for the hell of it.
I will become more of an independent thinker.
I will learn to say "pretty bird."
I will try to develop a taste for vegetables and grains.
I will add some new songs to my repertoire.
I will give my owners the gratitude and respect they deserve.
I will not frighten any more anthropologists.
I will increase my wheel-trotting speed to 250 r.p.m.
I will evolve.
R. Chast

ACCOUNTANT MANQUÉ

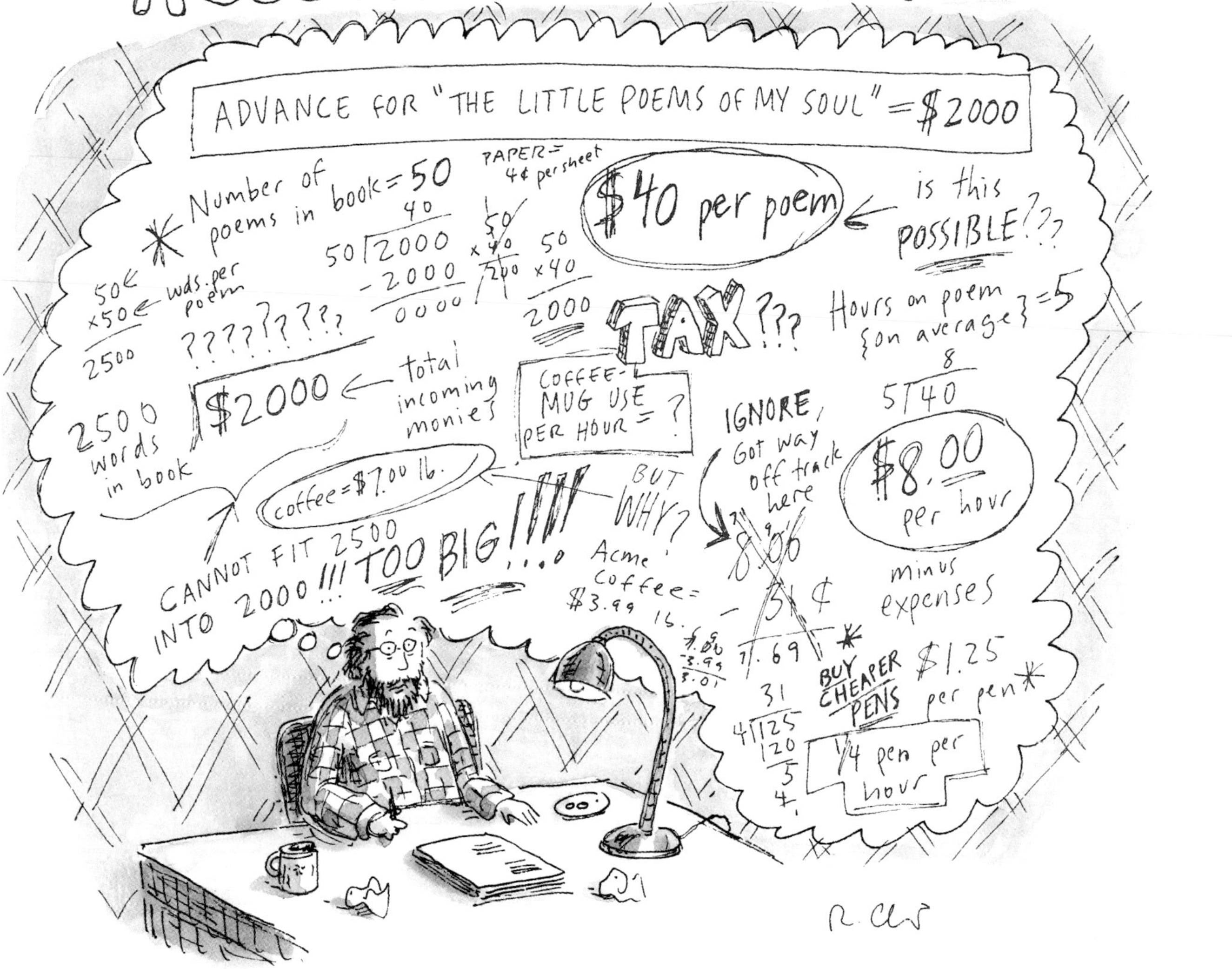
ADVANCE FOR "THE LITTLE POEMS OF MY SOUL" = $2000
Number of poems in book = 50
PAPER = 4¢ per sheet
$40 per poem
is this POSSIBLE???
50 wds. per poem
2500
????????
TAX???
Hours on poem {on average} = 5
2500 words in book
$2000
total incoming monies
COFFEE-MUG USE PER HOUR = ?
IGNORE, Got way off track here
$8.00 per hour
coffee = $7.00 lb.
BUT WHY?
CANNOT FIT 2500 INTO 2000!!! TOO BIG!!!!
Acme Coffee = $3.99 lb.
minus expenses
BUY CHEAPER PENS
$1.25 per pen
1/4 pen per hour

THE LAST FAMILY VACATION

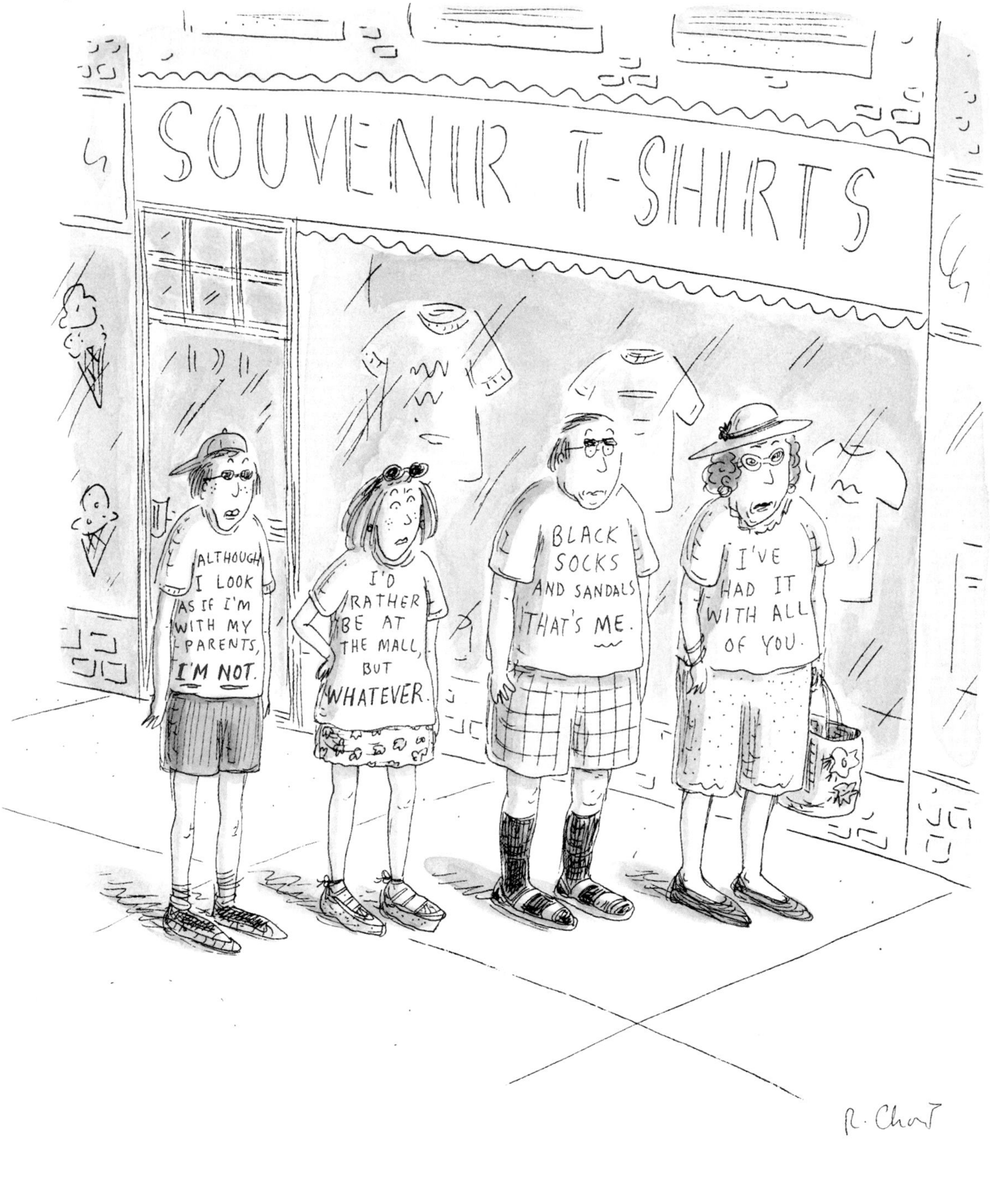
SOUVENIR T-SHIRTS
ALTHOUGH I LOOK AS IF I'M WITH MY PARENTS, I'M NOT.
I'D RATHER BE AT THE MALL, BUT WHATEVER.
BLACK SOCKS AND SANDALS THAT'S ME.
I'VE HAD IT WITH ALL OF YOU.
R. Chast

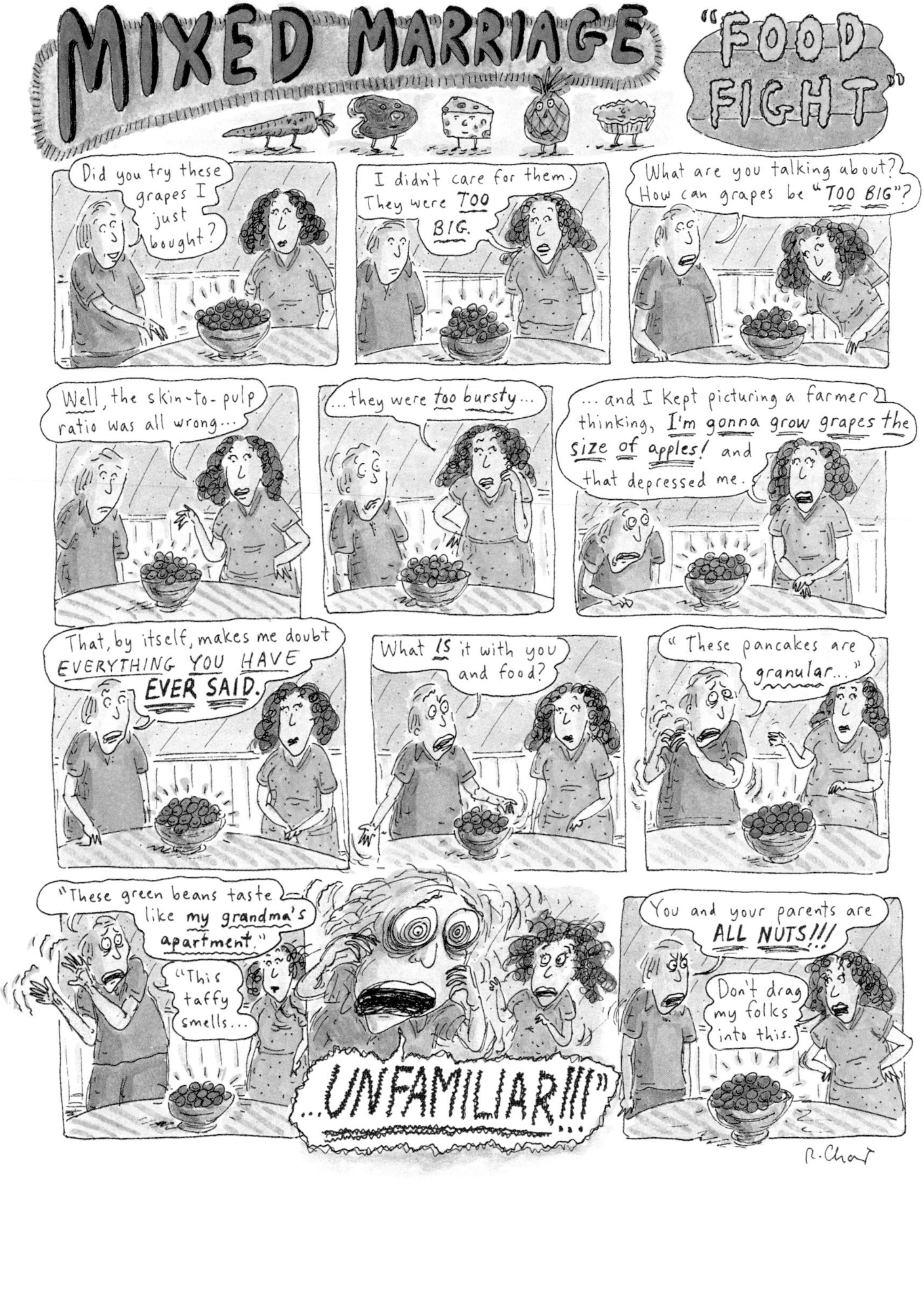
MIXED MARRIAGE
"FOOD FIGHT"
Did you try these grapes I just bought?
I didn't care for them. They were TOO BIG.
What are you talking about? How can grapes be "TOO BIG"?
Well, the skin-to-pulp ratio was all wrong...
...they were too bursty...
...and I kept picturing a farmer thinking, I'm gonna grow grapes the size of apples! and that depressed me.
That, by itself, makes me doubt EVERYTHING YOU HAVE EVER SAID.
What IS it with you and food?
"These pancakes are granular..."
"These green beans taste like my grandma's apartment."
"This taffy smells...
...UNFAMILIAR!!!"
You and your parents are ALL NUTS!!!
Don't drag my folks into this.
R. Chast

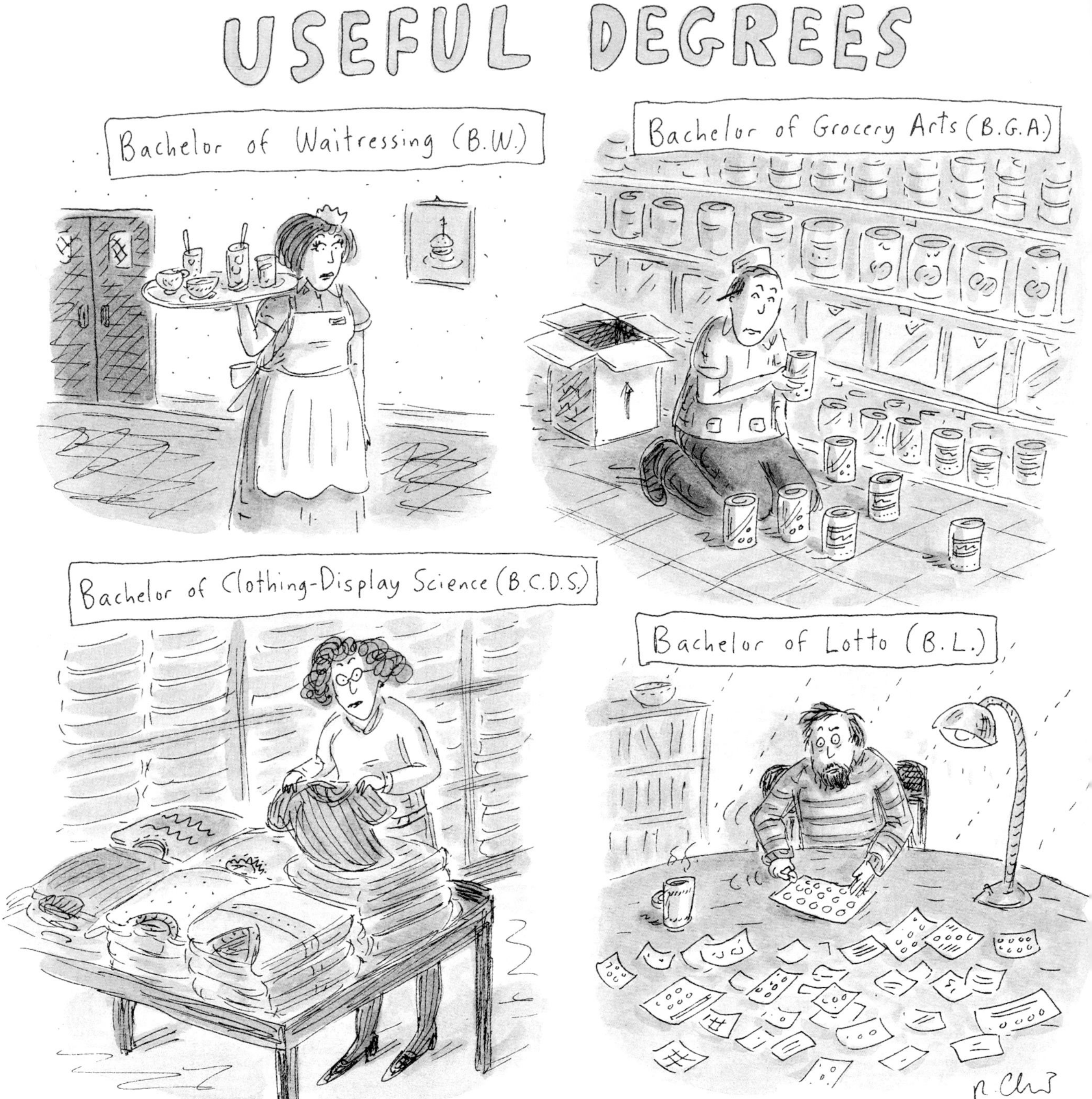
USEFUL DEGREES
Bachelor of Waitressing (B.W.)
Bachelor of Grocery Arts (B.G.A.)
Bachelor of Clothing-Display Science (B.C.D.S.)
Bachelor of Lotto (B.L.)

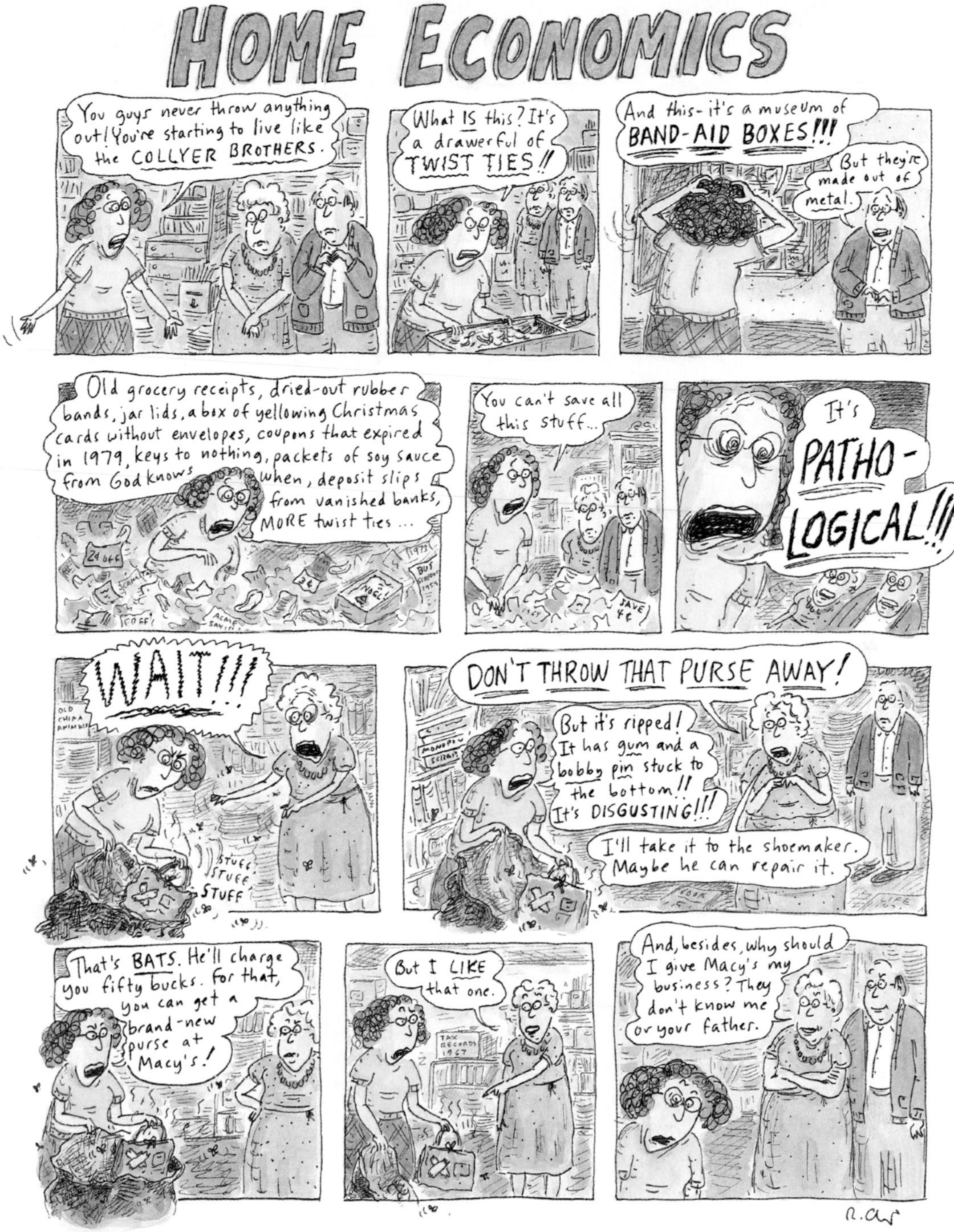
HOME ECONOMICS
You guys never throw anything out! You're starting to live like the COLLYER BROTHERS.
What IS this? It's a drawerful of TWIST TIES!!
And this- it's a museum of BAND-AID BOXES!!!
But they're made out of metal.
Old grocery receipts, dried-out rubber bands, jar lids, a box of yellowing Christmas cards without envelopes, coupons that expired in 1979, keys to nothing, packets of soy sauce from God knows when, deposit slips from vanished banks, MORE twist ties ...
You can't save all this stuff...
It's PATHO-LOGICAL!!!
WAIT!!!
STUFF STUFF STUFF
DON'T THROW THAT PURSE AWAY!
But it's ripped! It has gum and a bobby pin stuck to the bottom!! It's DISGUSTING!!!
I'll take it to the shoemaker. Maybe he can repair it.
That's BATS. He'll charge you fifty bucks. For that, you can get a brand-new purse at Macy's!
But I LIKE that one.
TAX RECORDS 1967
And, besides, why should I give Macy's my business? They don't know me or your father.
R.Ch

THE BOOK OF MILLIE

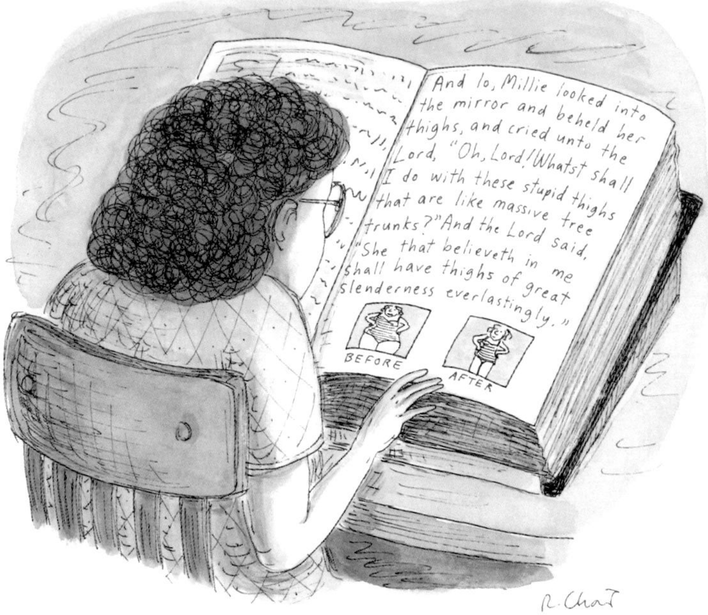
And lo, Millie looked into the mirror and beheld her thighs, and cried unto the Lord, "Oh, Lord! Whatst shall I do with these stupid thighs that are like massive tree trunks?" And the Lord said, "She that believeth in me shall have thighs of great slenderness everlastingly."
BEFORE
AFTER

THIRD-FLOOR RAPUNZEL

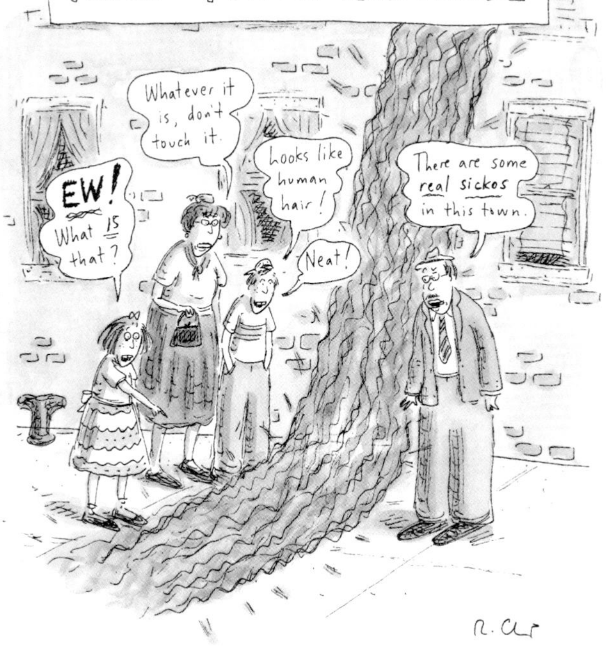
EW! What IS that?
Whatever it is, don't touch it.
Looks like human hair!
Neat!
There are some real sickos in this town.

A NURSERY RHYME FROM THE AMERICAN PSYCHIATRIC SOCIETY

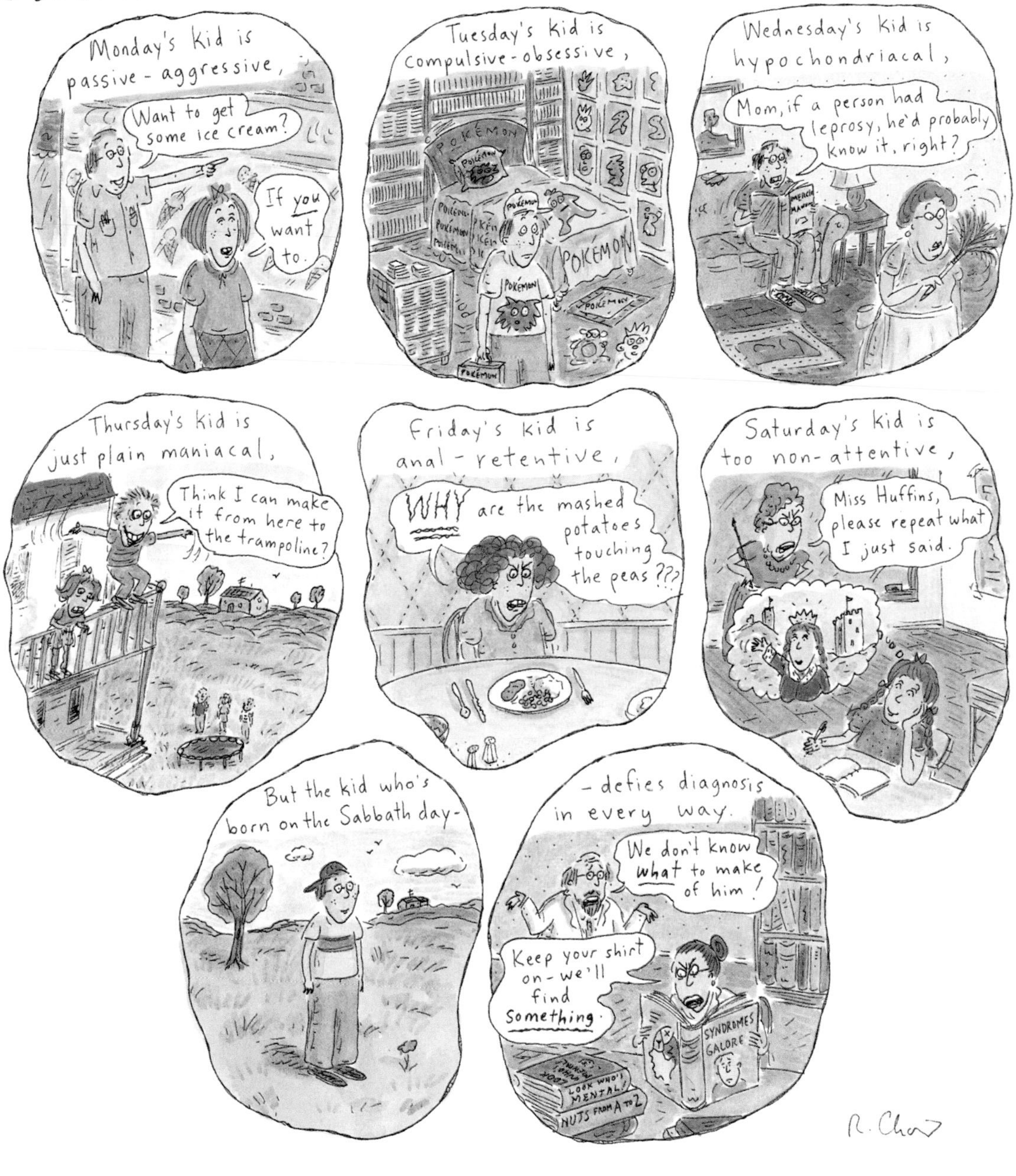

Monday's kid is passive-aggressive,
Want to get some ice cream?
If you want to.
Tuesday's kid is compulsive-obsessive,
POKÉMON
Wednesday's kid is hypochondriacal,
Mom, if a person had leprosy, he'd probably know it, right?
Thursday's kid is just plain maniacal,
Think I can make it from here to the trampoline?
Friday's kid is anal-retentive,
WHY are the mashed potatoes touching the peas???
Saturday's kid is too non-attentive,
Miss Huffins, please repeat what I just said.
But the kid who's born on the Sabbath day-
-defies diagnosis in every way.
We don't know what to make of him!
Keep your shirt on-we'll find something.
SYNDROMES GALORE
LOOK WHO'S MENTAL
NUTS FROM A TO Z
R. Chast

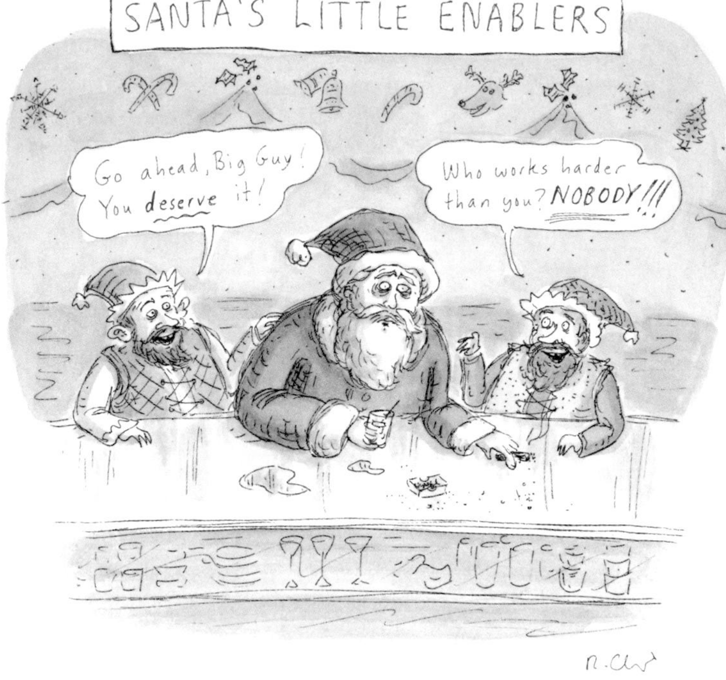
SANTA'S LITTLE ENABLERS
Go ahead, Big Guy! You deserve it!
Who works harder than you? NOBODY!!!

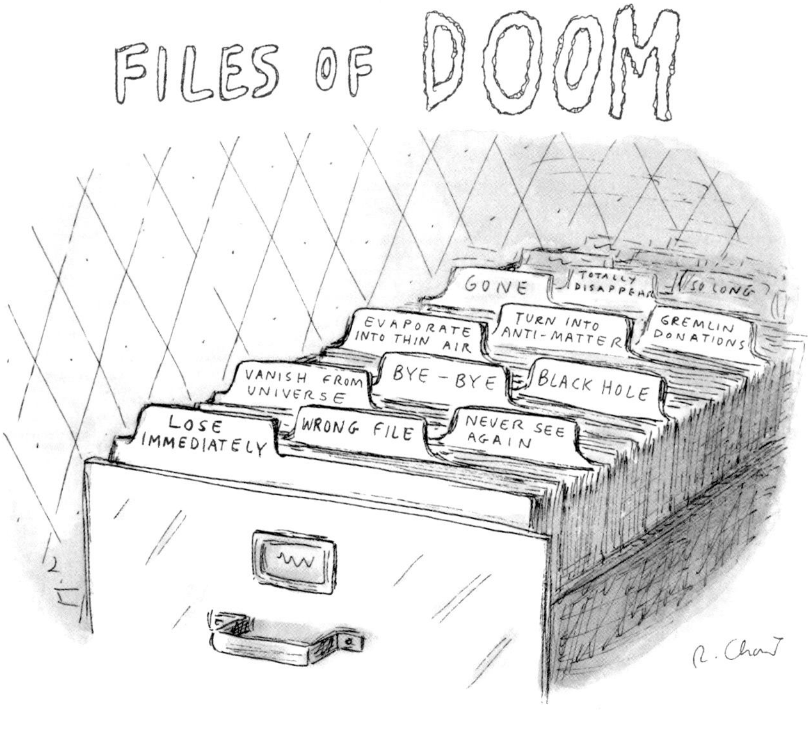
FILES OF DOOM
GONE
TOTALLY DISAPPEAR
SO LONG
EVAPORATE INTO THIN AIR
TURN INTO ANTI-MATTER
GREMLIN DONATIONS
VANISH FROM UNIVERSE
BYE-BYE
BLACK HOLE
LOSE IMMEDIATELY
WRONG FILE
NEVER SEE AGAIN

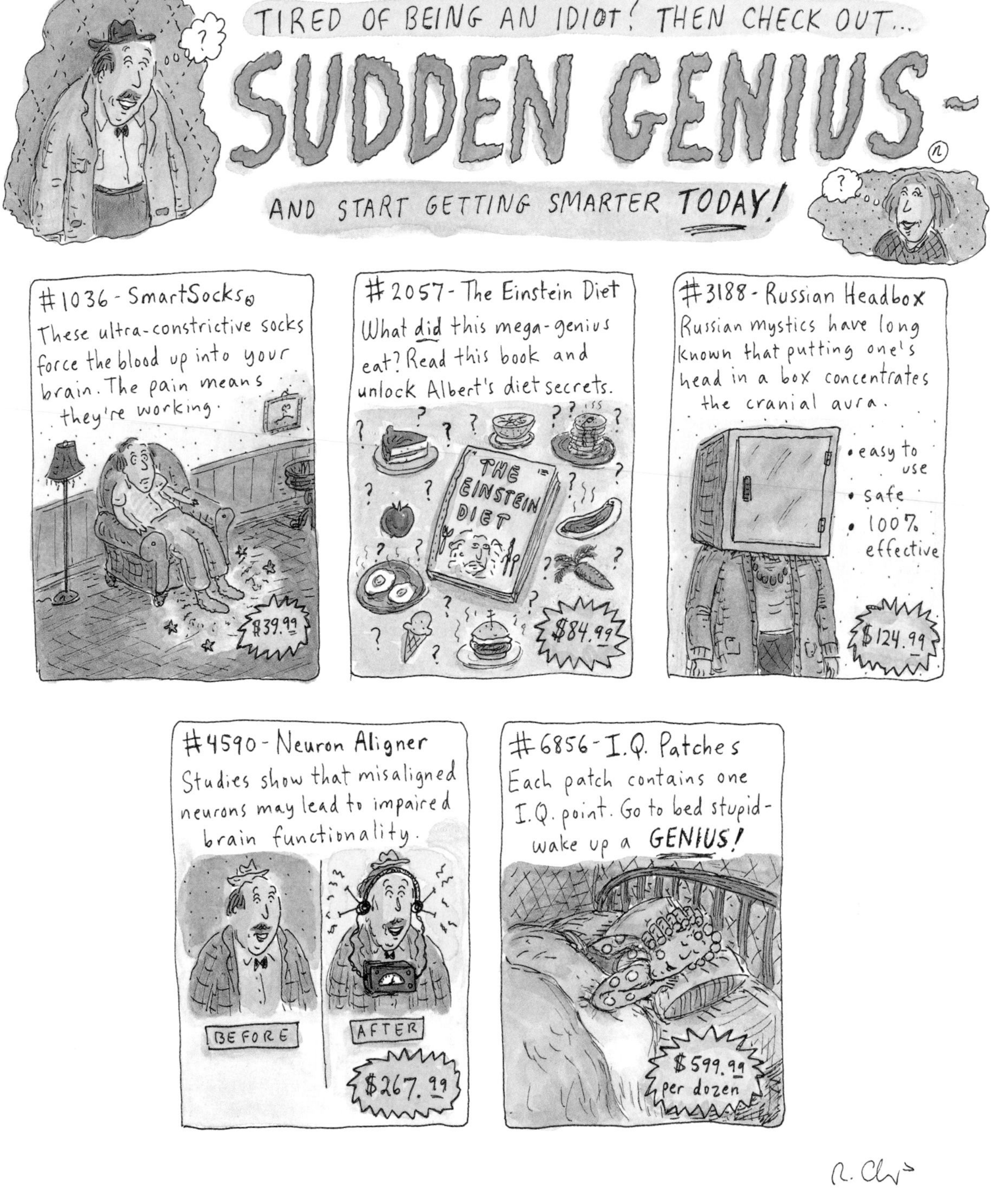
TIRED OF BEING AN IDIOT? THEN CHECK OUT...
SUDDEN GENIUS
AND START GETTING SMARTER TODAY!
#1036 - SmartSocks
These ultra-constrictive socks force the blood up into your brain. The pain means they're working.
$39.99
#2057 - The Einstein Diet
What did this mega-genius eat? Read this book and unlock Albert's diet secrets.
THE EINSTEIN DIET
$84.99
#3188 - Russian Headbox
Russian mystics have long known that putting one's head in a box concentrates the cranial aura.
• easy to use
• safe
• 100% effective
$124.99
#4590 - Neuron Aligner
Studies show that misaligned neurons may lead to impaired brain functionality.
BEFORE
AFTER
$267.99
#6856 - I.Q. Patches
Each patch contains one I.Q. point. Go to bed stupid - wake up a GENIUS!
$599.99 per dozen
R. Chast

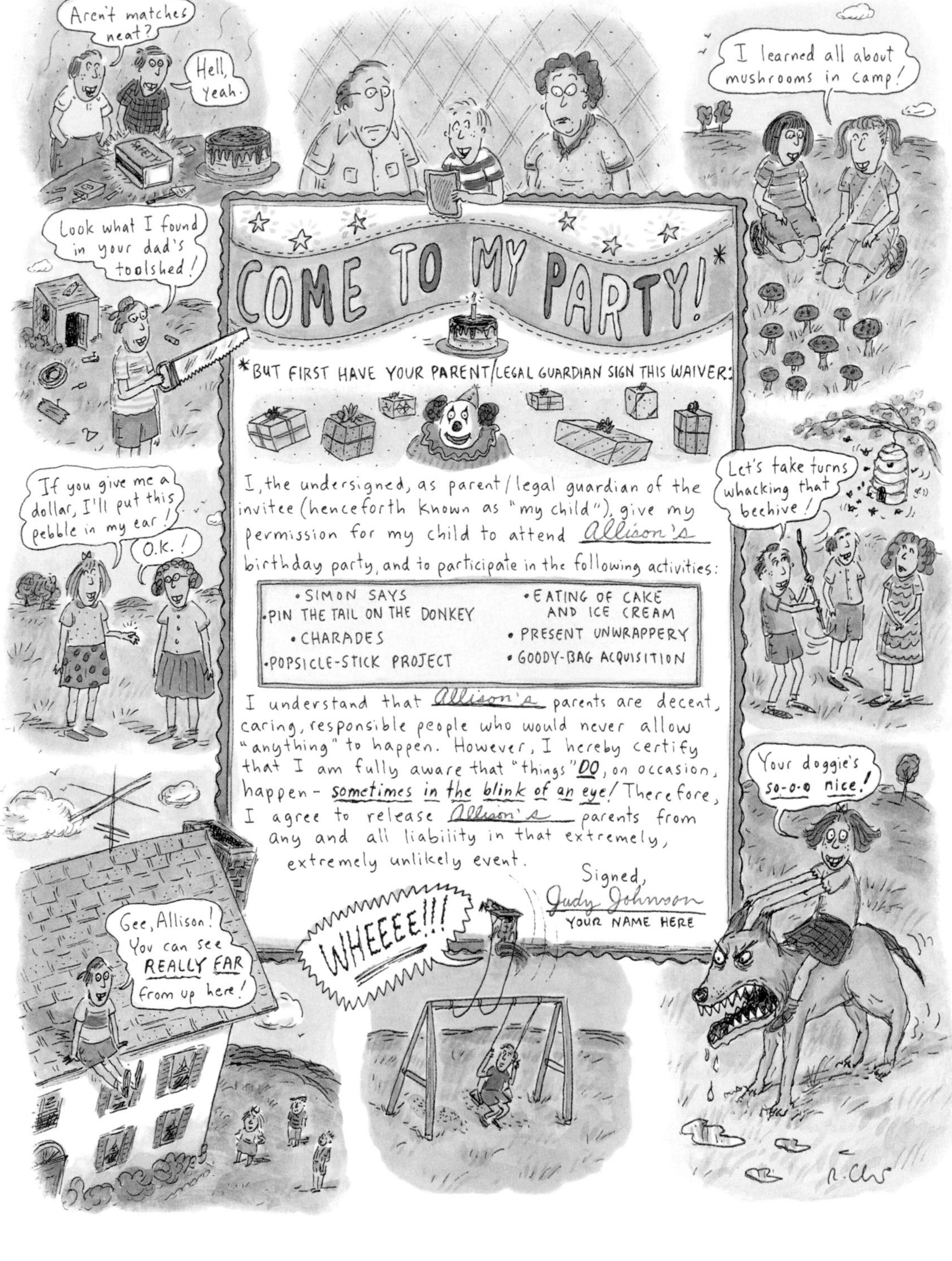

Aren't matches neat?
Hell, Yeah.
SAFETY
I learned all about mushrooms in camp!
Look what I found in your dad's toolshed!
COME TO MY PARTY!*
*BUT FIRST HAVE YOUR PARENT/LEGAL GUARDIAN SIGN THIS WAIVER:
I, the undersigned, as parent/legal guardian of the invitee (henceforth known as "my child"), give my permission for my child to attend Allison's birthday party, and to participate in the following activities:
• SIMON SAYS
• PIN THE TAIL ON THE DONKEY
• CHARADES
• POPSICLE-STICK PROJECT
• EATING OF CAKE AND ICE CREAM
• PRESENT UNWRAPPERY
• GOODY-BAG ACQUISITION
I understand that Allison's parents are decent, caring, responsible people who would never allow "anything" to happen. However, I hereby certify that I am fully aware that "things" DO, on occasion, happen - sometimes in the blink of an eye! Therefore, I agree to release Allison's parents from any and all liability in that extremely, extremely unlikely event.
Signed,
Judy Johnson
YOUR NAME HERE
If you give me a dollar, I'll put this pebble in my ear!
O.K.!
Let's take turns whacking that beehive!
Your doggie's so-o-o nice!
Gee, Allison! You can see REALLY FAR from up here!
WHEEEE!!!
R. Chast

IN A JUST WORLD

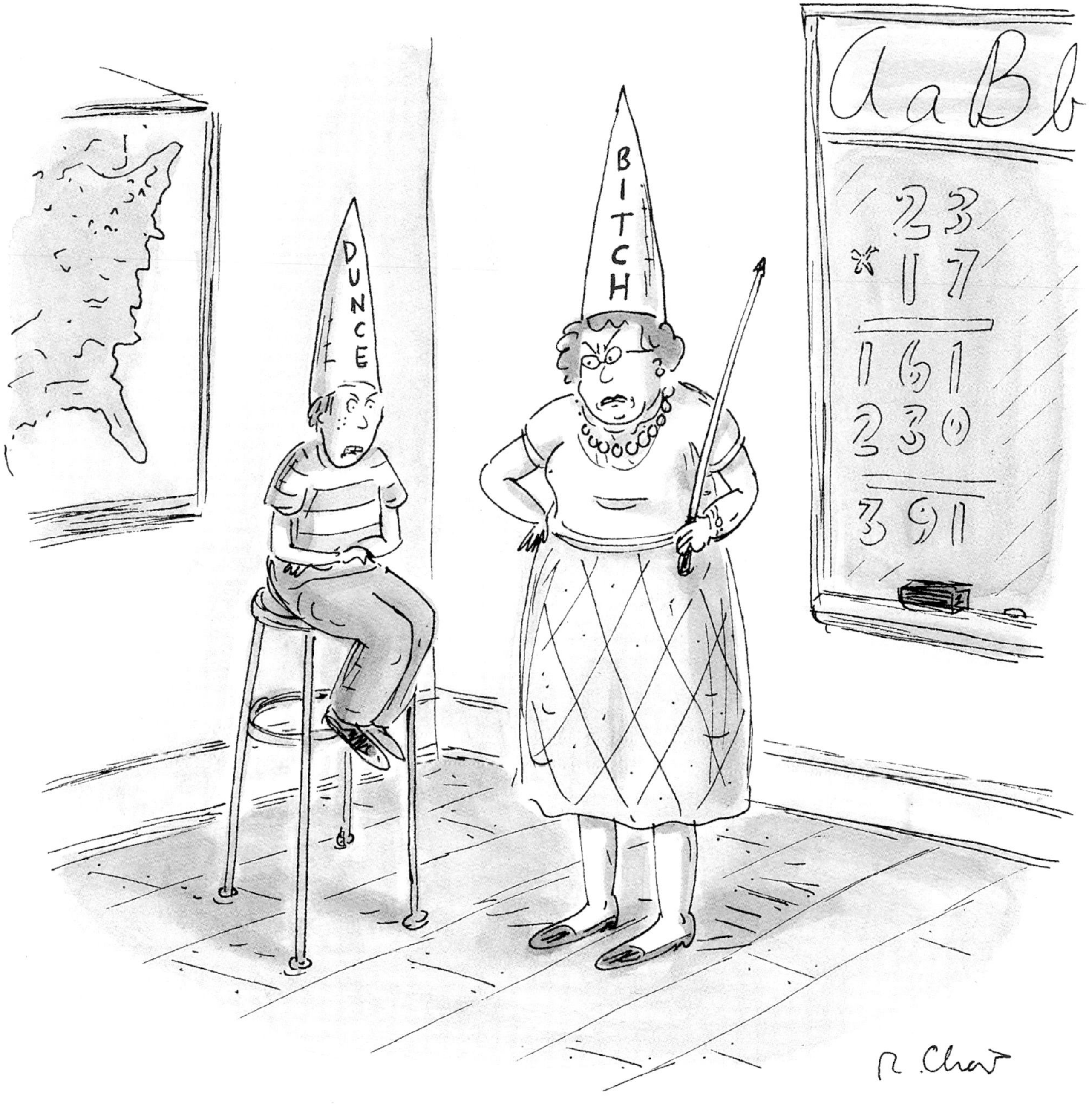

DUNCE
BITCH
AaBb
23
× 17
161
230
391
R. Chast

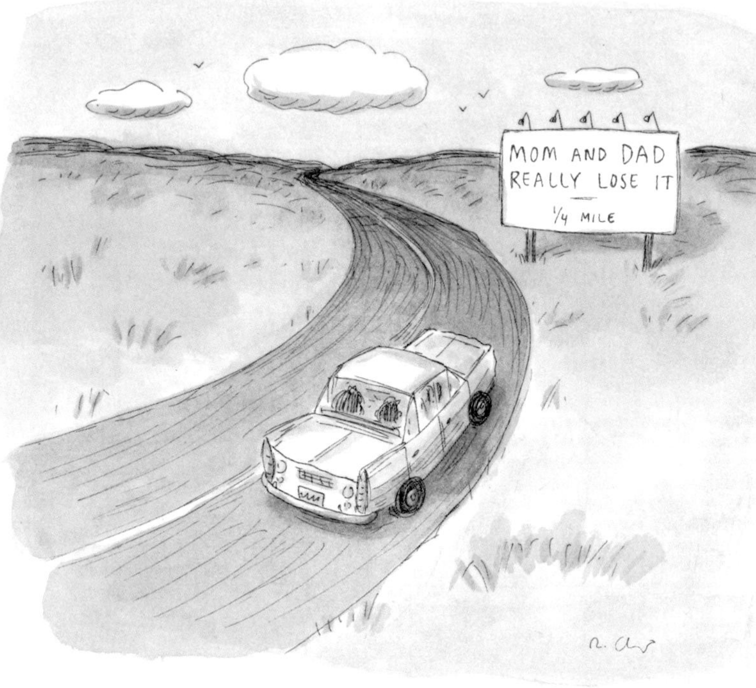
MOM AND DAD
REALLY LOSE IT
1/4 MILE

NONMEDICAL-ALERT BRACELETS

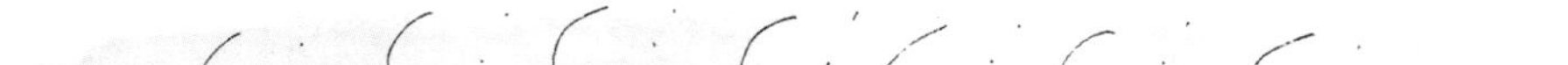
MARY JANE FLECK
DO NOT EXPOSE TO COUNTRY-WESTERN MUSIC
BARNEY BALLENS
EXTREMELY SENSITIVE TO CHINTZ
PHILIP PEETS
ALLERGIC TO ALGEBRA
MINDY NARNSWORTH
PARALLEL-PARKING INTOLERANT
Cal Chorney-Otis
Household chores may cause fatal reaction

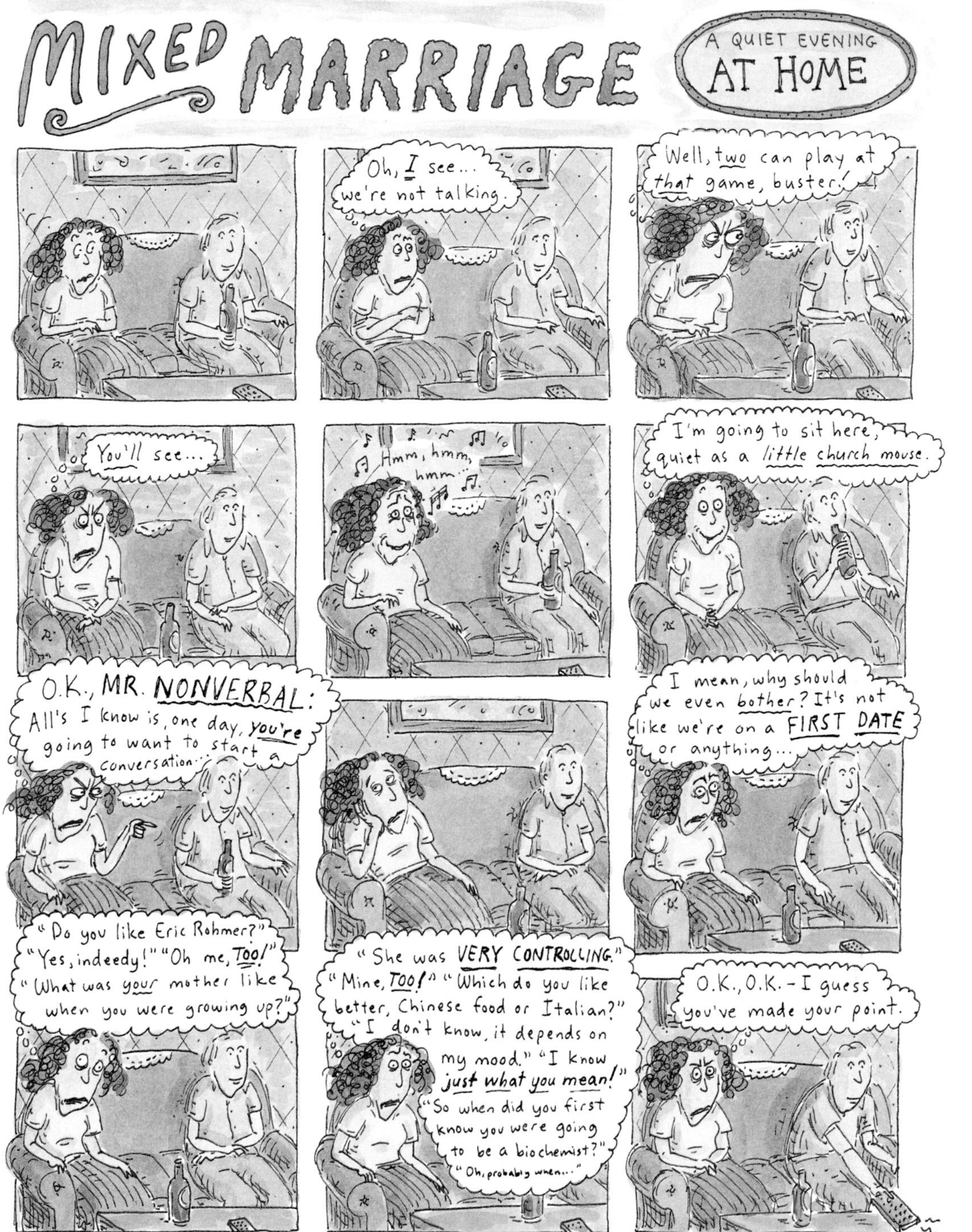
MIXED MARRIAGE
A QUIET EVENING AT HOME
Oh, I see... we're not talking.
Well, two can play at that game, buster!
You'll see...
Hmm, hmm, hmm...
I'm going to sit here, quiet as a little church mouse.
O.K., MR. NONVERBAL: All's I know is, one day, you're going to want to start a conversation...
I mean, why should we even bother? It's not like we're on a FIRST DATE or anything...
"Do you like Eric Rohmer?" "Yes, indeedy!" "Oh me, TOO!" "What was your mother like when you were growing up?"
"She was VERY CONTROLLING." "Mine, TOO!" "Which do you like better, Chinese food or Italian?" "I don't know, it depends on my mood." "I know just what you mean!" "So when did you first know you were going to be a biochemist?" "Oh, probably when..."
O.K., O.K. - I guess you've made your point.
CLICK
R. Chast

THE CAB OF GUILT
This is your mother, reminding you that if you don't buckle up I will kill myself.

BOTOX THEATRE

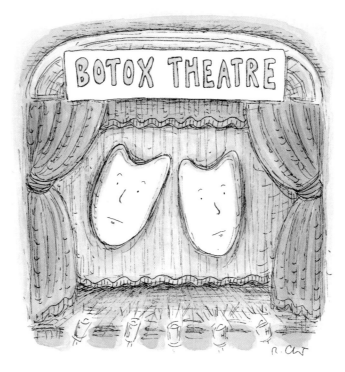

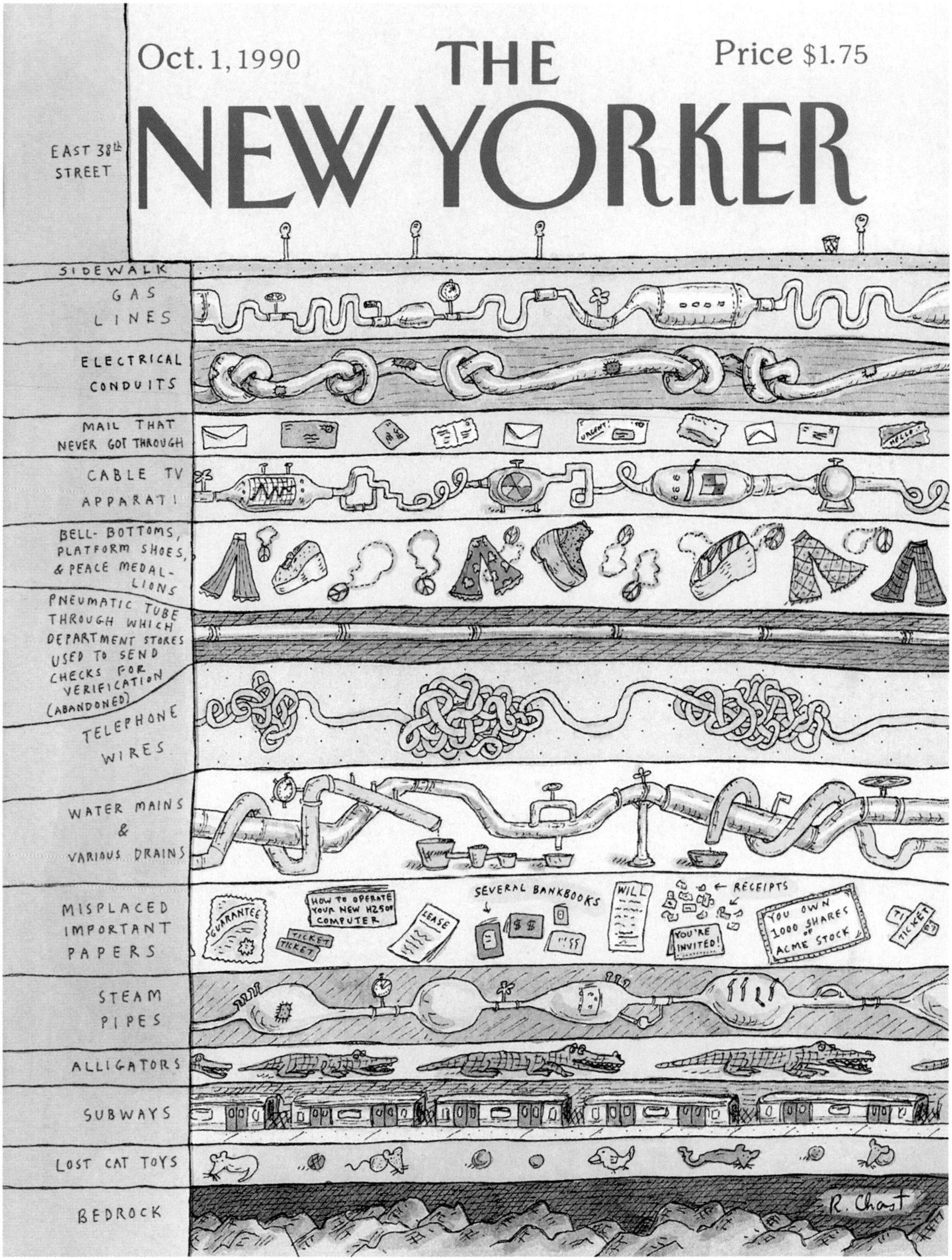
Oct. 1, 1990
THE NEW YORKER
Price $1.75
EAST 38th STREET
SIDEWALK
GAS LINES
ELECTRICAL CONDUITS
MAIL THAT NEVER GOT THROUGH
CABLE TV APPARATI
BELL-BOTTOMS, PLATFORM SHOES, & PEACE MEDAL-LIONS
PNEUMATIC TUBE THROUGH WHICH DEPARTMENT STORES USED TO SEND CHECKS FOR VERIFICATION (ABANDONED)
TELEPHONE WIRES
WATER MAINS & VARIOUS DRAINS
MISPLACED IMPORTANT PAPERS
GUARANTEE
HOW TO OPERATE YOUR NEW H250 COMPUTER
TICKET
TICKET
LEASE
SEVERAL BANKBOOKS
WILL
← RECEIPTS
YOU'RE INVITED!
YOU OWN 1000 SHARES OF ACME STOCK
TICKET
STEAM PIPES
ALLIGATORS
SUBWAYS
LOST CAT TOYS
BEDROCK
R. Chast

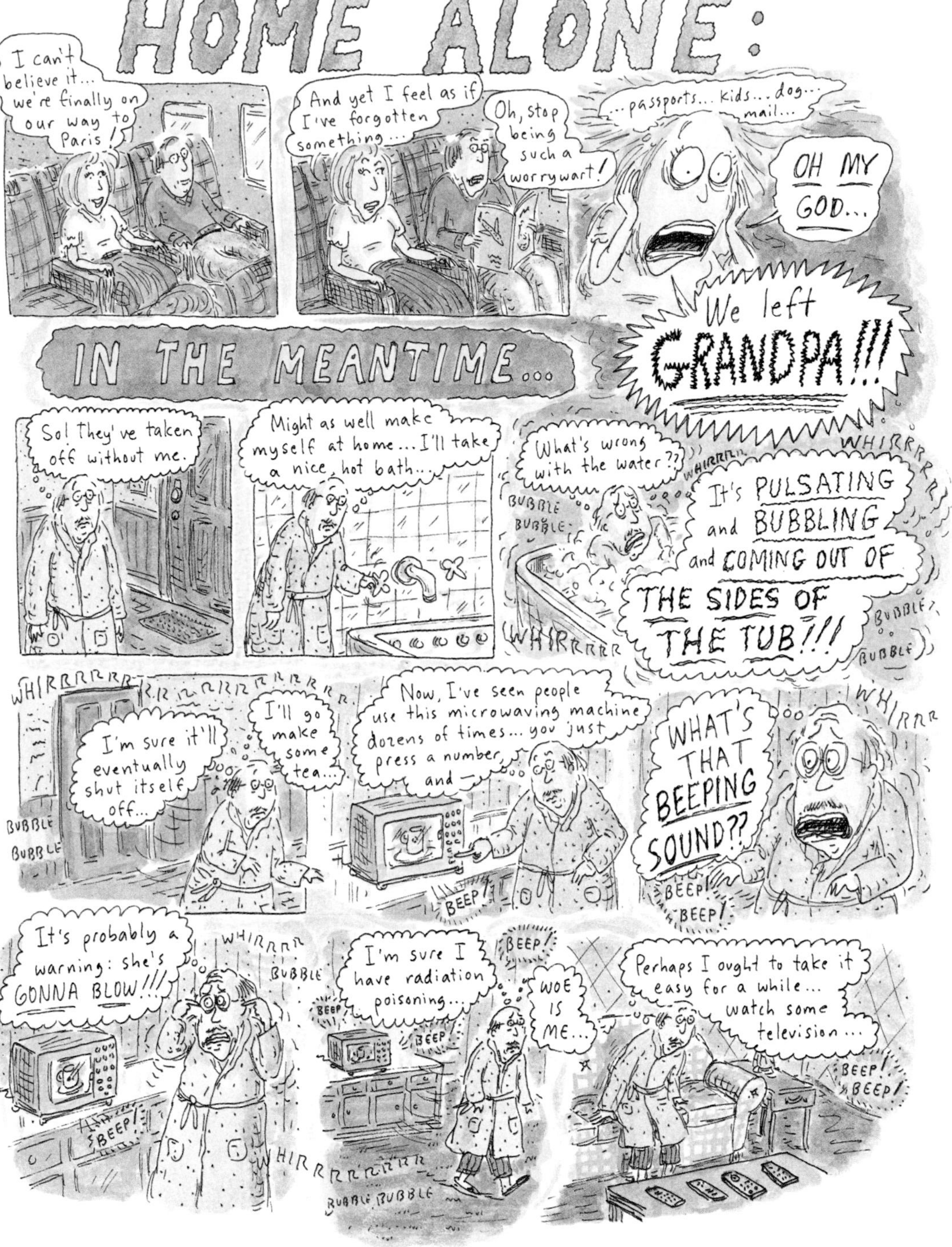
HOME ALONE:
I can't believe it... we're finally on our way to Paris!
And yet I feel as if I've forgotten something...
Oh, stop being such a worrywart!
...passports... kids... dog... mail...
OH MY GOD...
We left GRANDPA!!!
IN THE MEANTIME...
So! They've taken off without me.
Might as well make myself at home... I'll take a nice, hot bath...
What's wrong with the water??
WHIRRRRR
BUBBLE BUBBLE
It's PULSATING and BUBBLING and COMING OUT OF THE SIDES OF THE TUB!!!
WHIRRRRR
BUBBLE BUBBLE
WHIRRRRRRRRRRRRRRRRRR
I'm sure it'll eventually shut itself off...
BUBBLE BUBBLE
I'll go make some tea...
Now, I've seen people use this microwaving machine dozens of times... you just press a number, and—
BEEP!
WHAT'S THAT BEEPING SOUND??
WHIRRR
BEEP! BEEP!
It's probably a warning: she's GONNA BLOW!!!
WHIRRRRR BUBBLE
BEEP!
I'm sure I have radiation poisoning...
BEEP! BEEP! BEEP!
WOE IS ME...
WHIRRRRRRRRR
BUBBLE BUBBLE
Perhaps I ought to take it easy for a while... watch some television...
BEEP! BEEP!

The Final Chapter

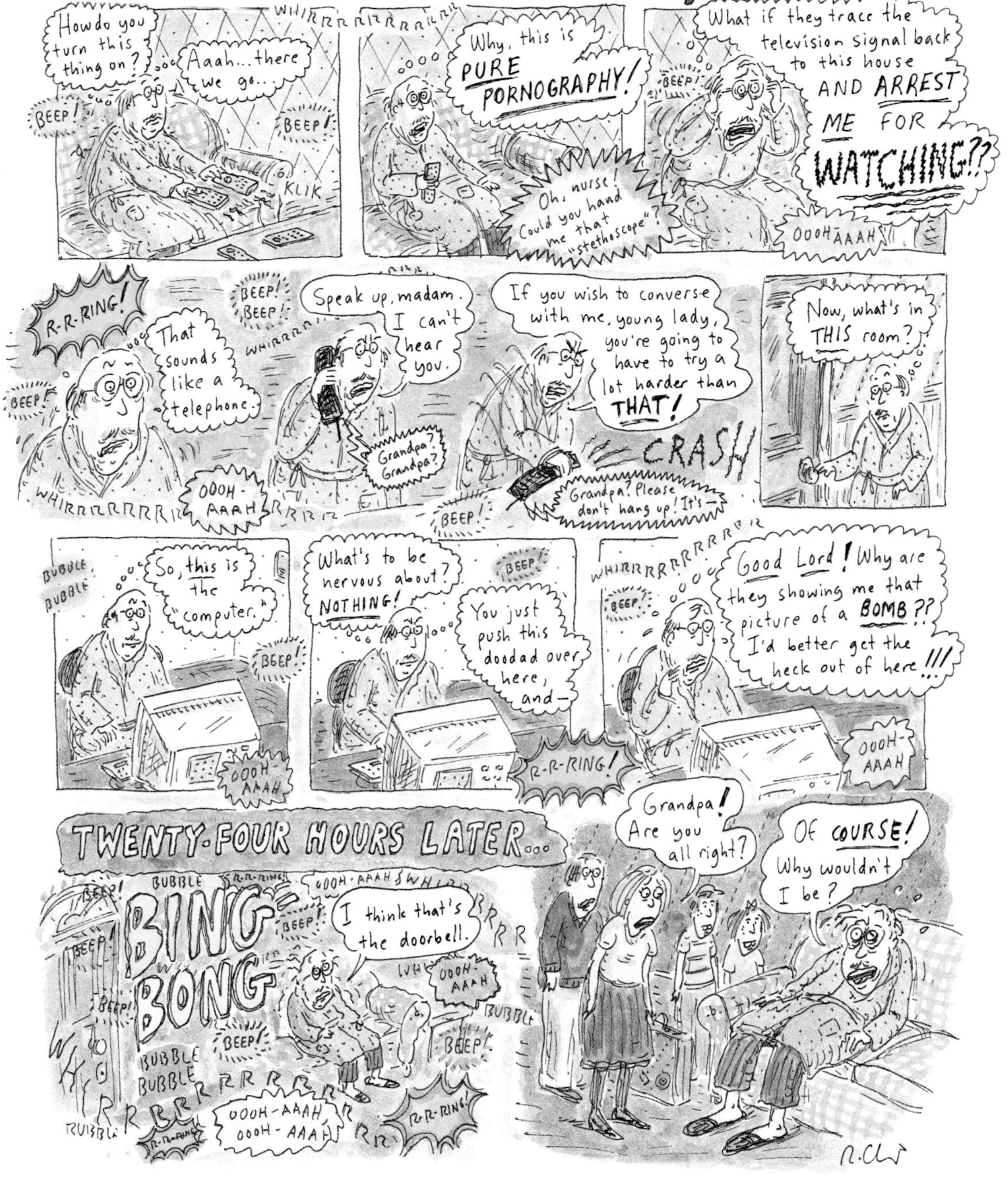
How do you turn this thing on?
BEEP!
Aaah... there we go...
BEEP!
KLIK
WHIRRRRRRRRRRRRRR
Why, this is PURE PORNOGRAPHY!
Oh, nurse! Could you hand me that "stethoscope"?
BEEP!
What if they trace the television signal back to this house AND ARREST ME FOR WATCHING??
OOOH-AAAH
R-R-RING!
BEEP!
That sounds like a telephone.
WHIRRRRRRRRRRR
OOOH-AAAH
BEEP! BEEP!
WHIRRRR
Speak up, madam. I can't hear you.
Grandpa? Grandpa?
If you wish to converse with me, young lady, you're going to have to try a lot harder than THAT!
CRASH
Grandpa? Please don't hang up! It's—
BEEP!
Now, what's in THIS room?
BUBBLE BUBBLE
So, this is the "computer."
BEEP!
OOOH-AAAH
What's to be nervous about? NOTHING!
BEEP!
You just push this doodad over here, and—
R-R-RING!
WHIRRRRRRRRRRR
BEEP!
Good Lord! Why are they showing me that picture of a BOMB?? I'd better get the heck out of here!!!
OOOH-AAAH
TWENTY-FOUR HOURS LATER...
BUBBLE
R-R-RING!
OOOH-AAAH
BEEP!
BING-BONG
I think that's the doorbell.
OOOH-AAAH
BEEP!
BUBBLE BUBBLE
BRRRRRRRRR
OOOH-AAAH, OOOH-AAAH
R-R-RING!
Grandpa! Are you all right?
OF COURSE! Why wouldn't I be?
R. Chast

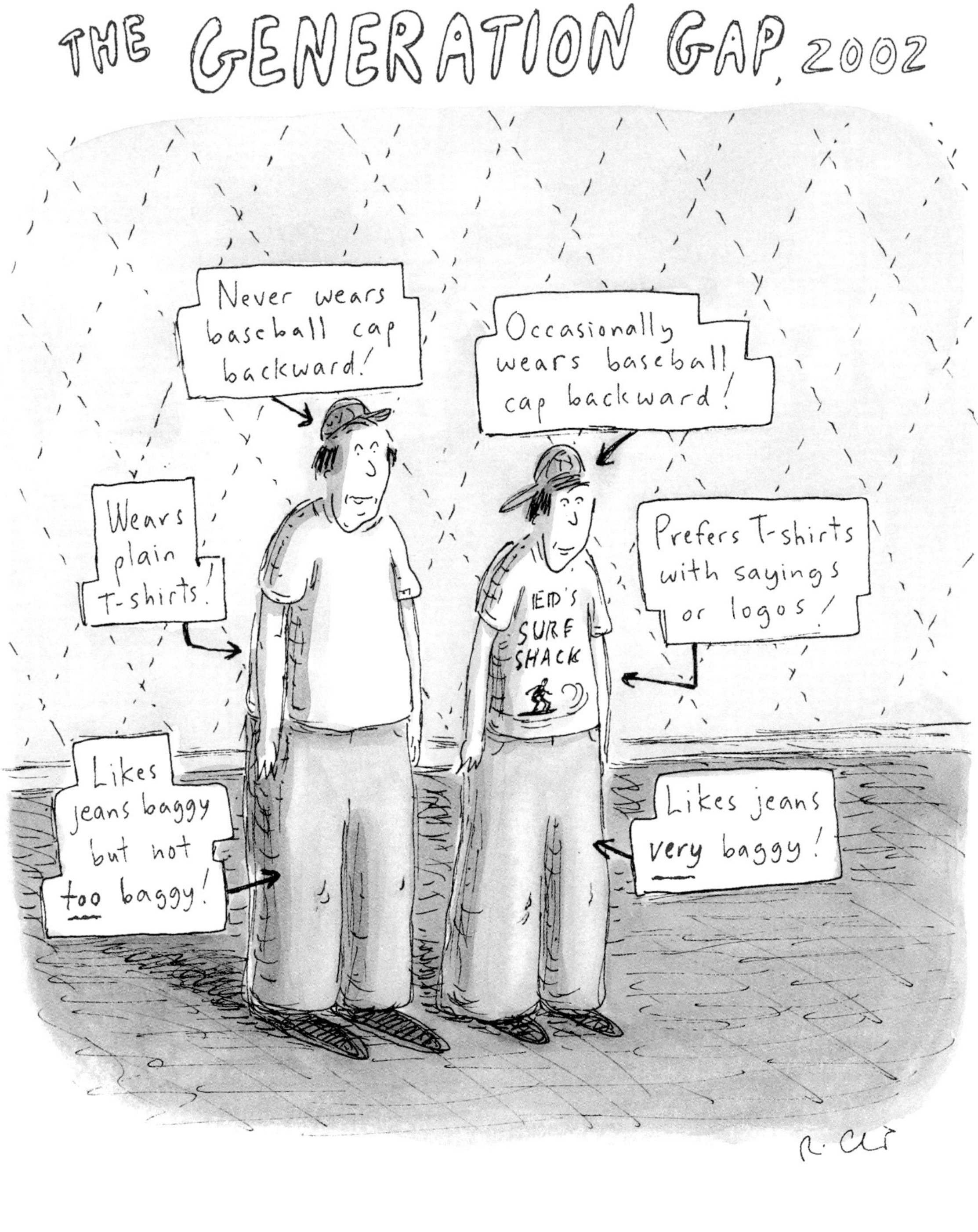
THE GENERATION GAP, 2002
Never wears baseball cap backward!
Occasionally wears baseball cap backward!
Wears plain T-shirts!
Prefers T-shirts with sayings or logos!
ED'S SURF SHACK
Likes jeans baggy but not too baggy!
Likes jeans very baggy!

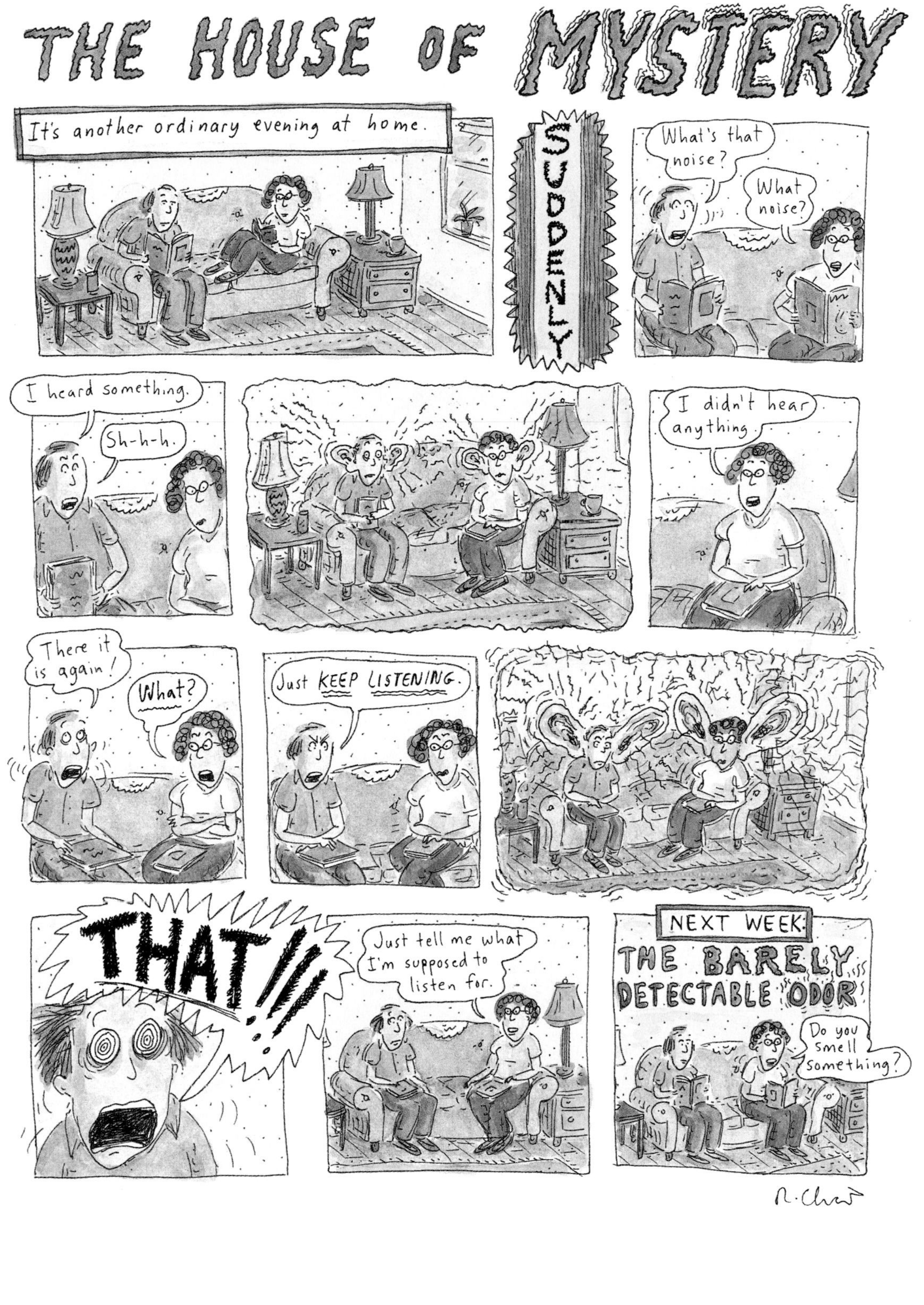
THE HOUSE OF MYSTERY
It's another ordinary evening at home.
SUDDENLY
What's that noise?
What noise?
I heard something.
Sh-h-h.
I didn't hear anything.
There it is again!
What?
Just KEEP LISTENING.
THAT!!!
Just tell me what I'm supposed to listen for.
NEXT WEEK:
THE BARELY DETECTABLE ODOR
Do you smell something?
R. Chast

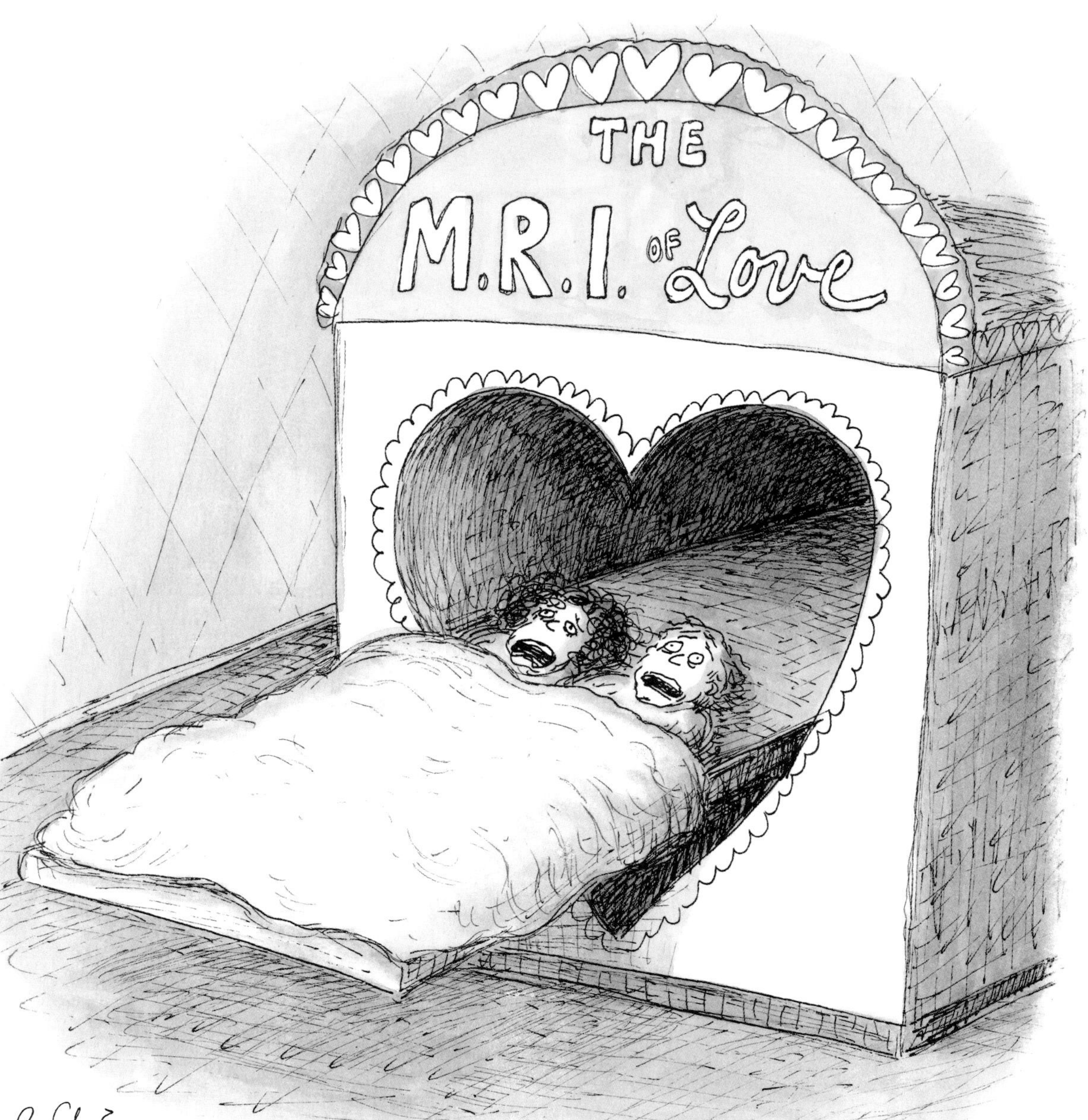
THE
M.R.I. OF Love

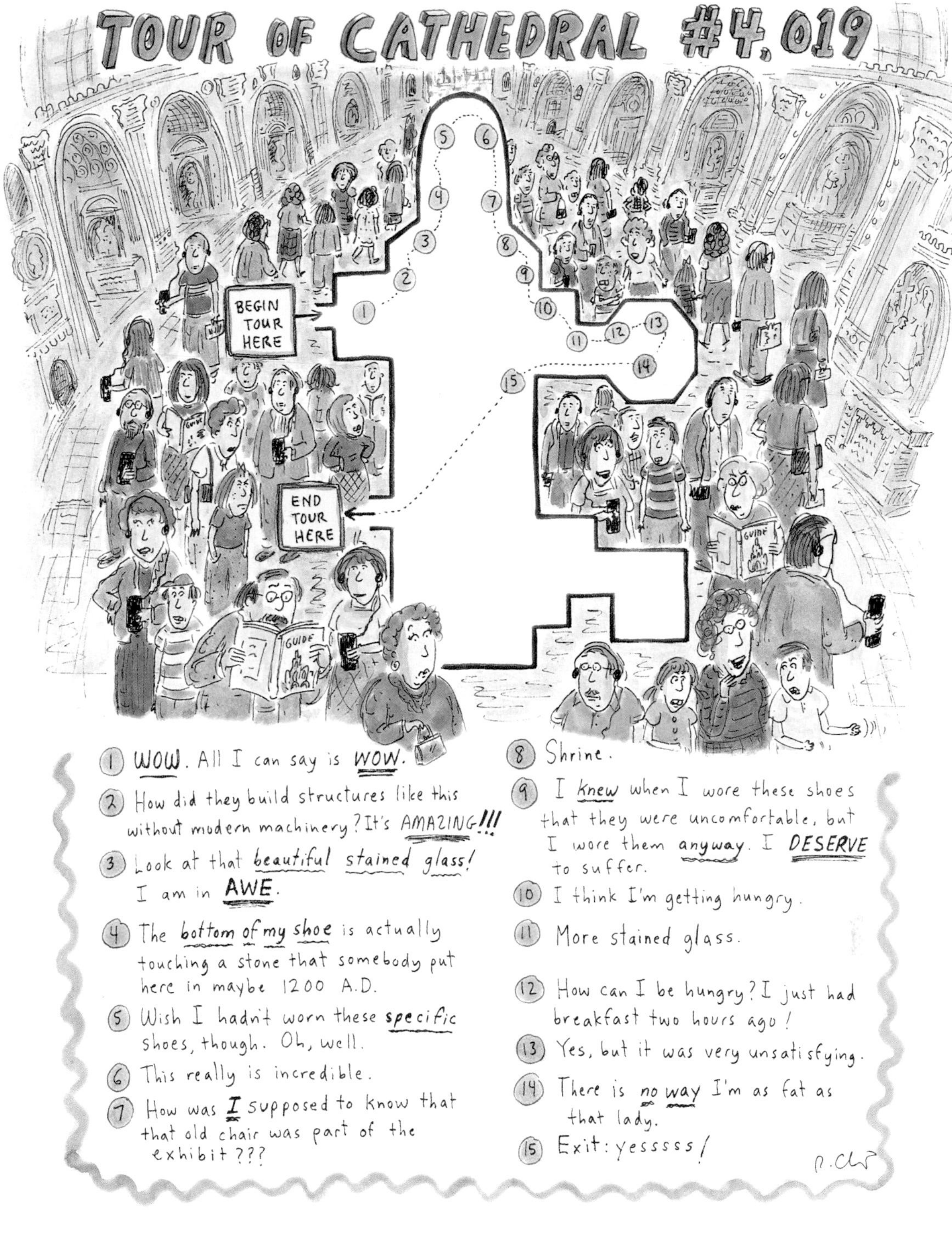
TOUR OF CATHEDRAL #4,019
BEGIN TOUR HERE
END TOUR HERE
GUIDE
1 WOW. All I can say is WOW.
2 How did they build structures like this without modern machinery? It's AMAZING!!!
3 Look at that beautiful stained glass! I am in AWE.
4 The bottom of my shoe is actually touching a stone that somebody put here in maybe 1200 A.D.
5 Wish I hadn't worn these specific shoes, though. Oh, well.
6 This really is incredible.
7 How was I supposed to know that that old chair was part of the exhibit???
8 Shrine.
9 I knew when I wore these shoes that they were uncomfortable, but I wore them anyway. I DESERVE to suffer.
10 I think I'm getting hungry.
11 More stained glass.
12 How can I be hungry? I just had breakfast two hours ago!
13 Yes, but it was very unsatisfying.
14 There is no way I'm as fat as that lady.
15 Exit: yessss!

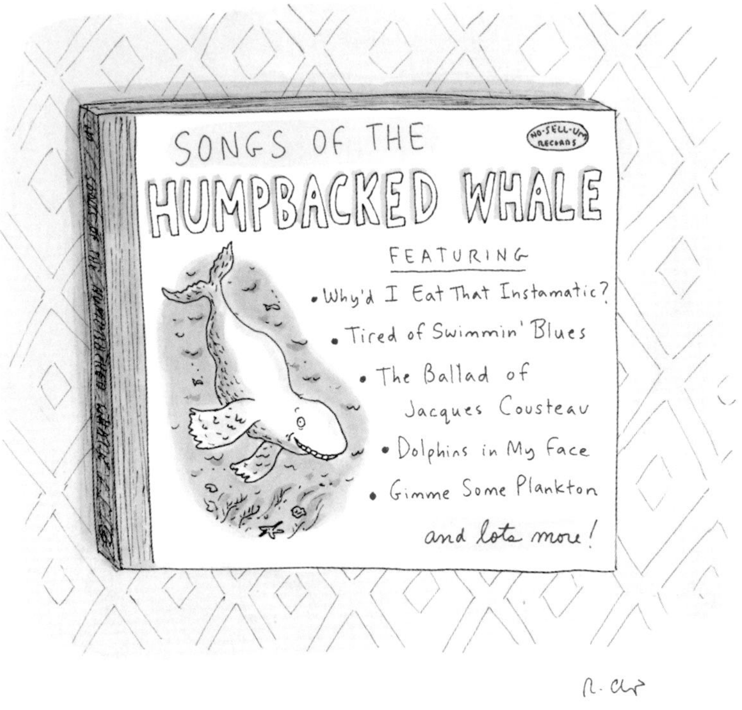
SONGS OF THE
HUMPBACKED WHALE
NO-SELL-UM RECORDS
FEATURING
• Why'd I Eat That Instamatic?
• Tired of Swimmin' Blues
• The Ballad of Jacques Cousteau
• Dolphins in My Face
• Gimme Some Plankton
and lots more!

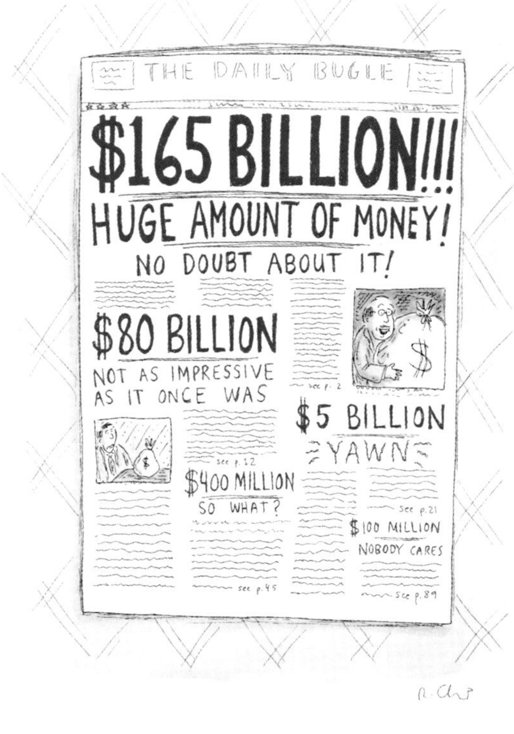
THE DAILY BUGLE
$165 BILLION!!!
HUGE AMOUNT OF MONEY!
NO DOUBT ABOUT IT!
$80 BILLION
NOT AS IMPRESSIVE AS IT ONCE WAS
see p. 2
$5 BILLION
YAWN
see p. 12
$400 MILLION
SO WHAT?
see p. 21
$100 MILLION
NOBODY CARES
see p. 45
see p. 89

UNUSUAL RETIREMENT PLANS

1000-F.A.I.

I'll take a thousand bucks, stick it in a bank, "forget about it," and in thirty years I'll be pleasantly surprised.

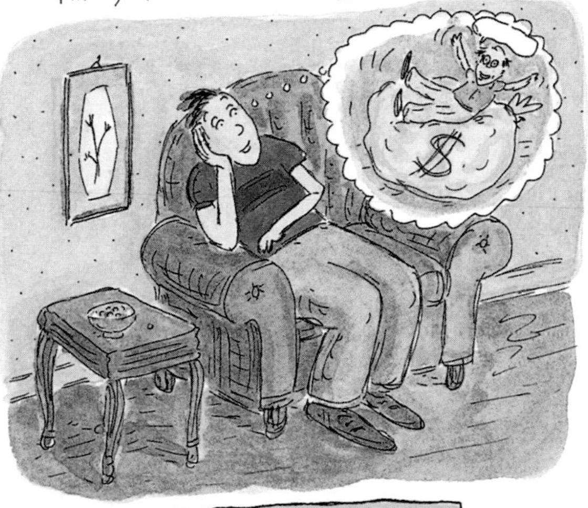

M.K. Plan

"My Kids" will take care of me. I'm virtually certain of that.

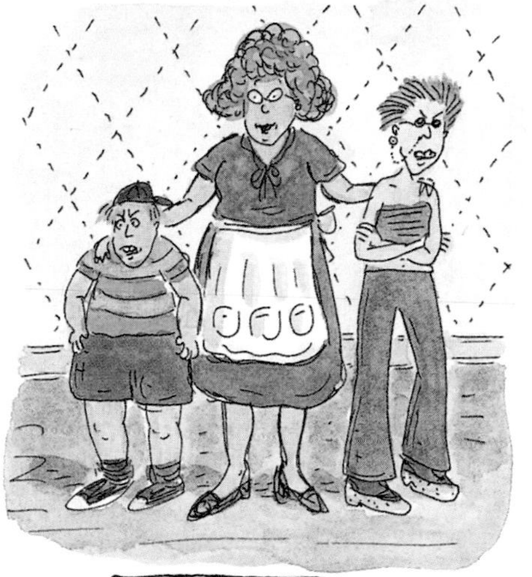

Jackpot Account

I'm not going to need one, because I'm going to be RICH, yessirree Bob.

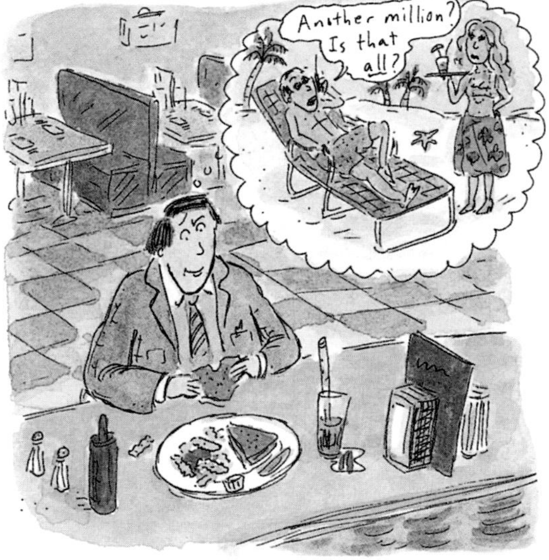
Another million? Is that all?

The ? Plan

Who can plan, like, next week? Because an asteroid could smash into the Earth tomorrow, so what's the point?

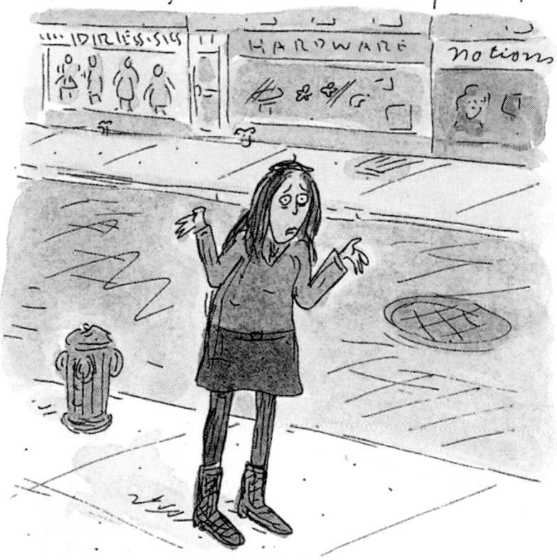
DRESSES
HARDWARE
notions

THE DREAM REMOTE

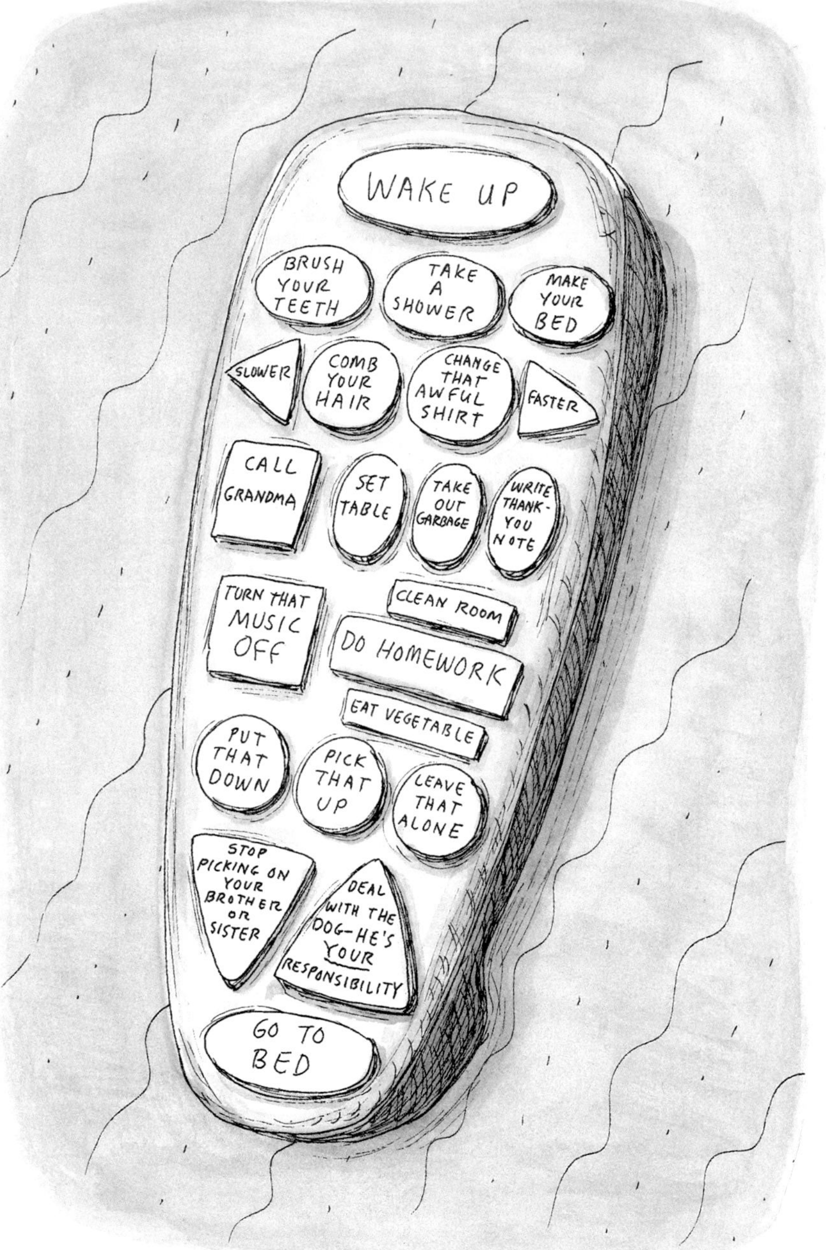
WAKE UP
BRUSH YOUR TEETH
TAKE A SHOWER
MAKE YOUR BED
SLOWER
COMB YOUR HAIR
CHANGE THAT AWFUL SHIRT
FASTER
CALL GRANDMA
SET TABLE
TAKE OUT GARBAGE
WRITE THANK-YOU NOTE
TURN THAT MUSIC OFF
CLEAN ROOM
DO HOMEWORK
EAT VEGETABLE
PUT THAT DOWN
PICK THAT UP
LEAVE THAT ALONE
STOP PICKING ON YOUR BROTHER OR SISTER
DEAL WITH THE DOG—HE'S YOUR RESPONSIBILITY
GO TO BED
R. Chast

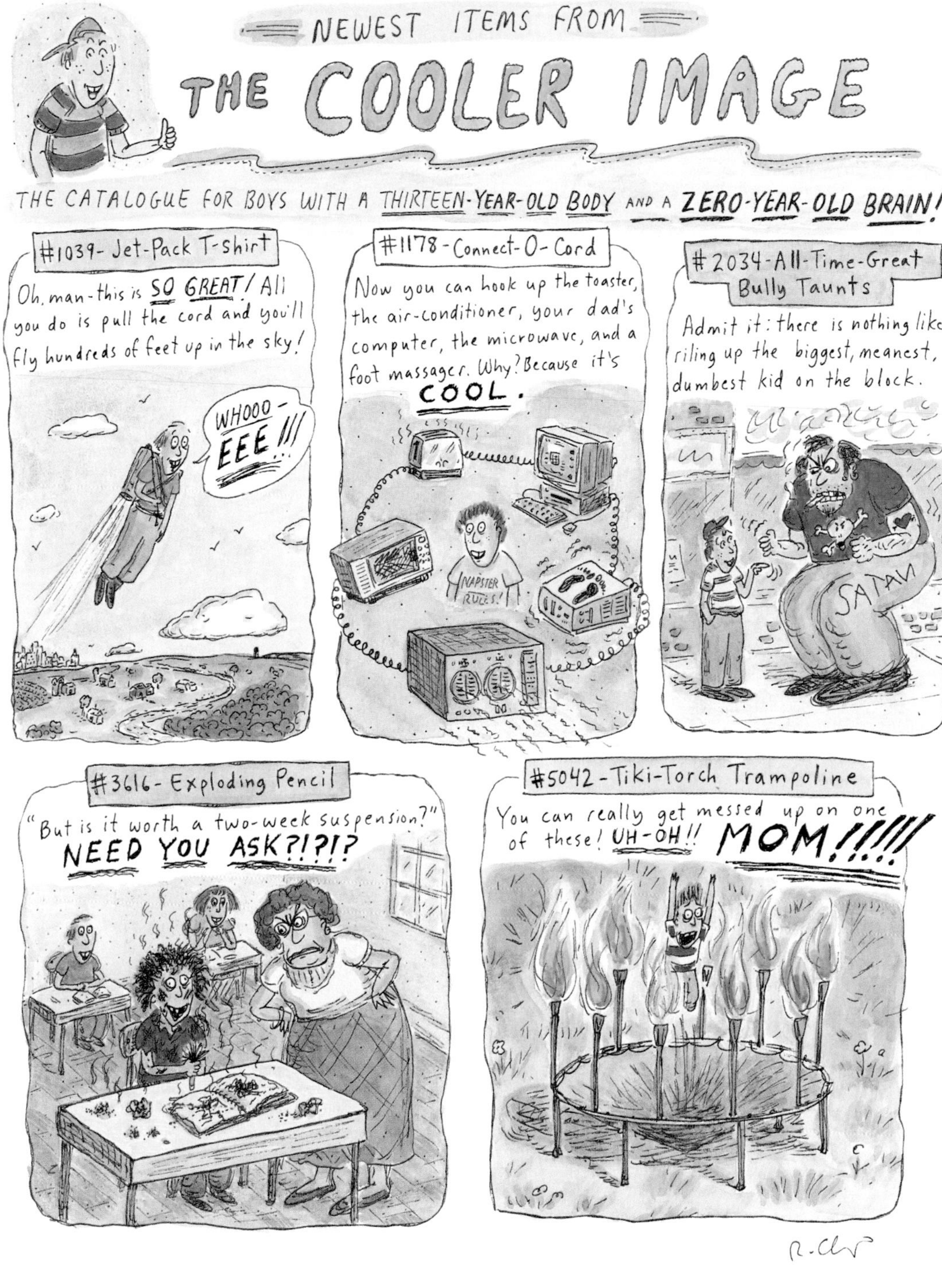
NEWEST ITEMS FROM
THE COOLER IMAGE
THE CATALOGUE FOR BOYS WITH A THIRTEEN-YEAR-OLD BODY AND A ZERO-YEAR-OLD BRAIN!
#1039- Jet-Pack T-shirt
Oh, man-this is SO GREAT! All you do is pull the cord and you'll fly hundreds of feet up in the sky!
WHOOO-EEE!!!
#1178-Connect-O-Cord
Now you can hook up the toaster, the air-conditioner, your dad's computer, the microwave, and a foot massager. Why? Because it's COOL.
NAPSTER RULES!
#2034-All-Time-Great Bully Taunts
Admit it: there is nothing like riling up the biggest, meanest, dumbest kid on the block.
SATAN
#3616-Exploding Pencil
"But is it worth a two-week suspension?" NEED YOU ASK?!?!?
#5042-Tiki-Torch Trampoline
You can really get messed up on one of these! UH-OH!! MOM!!!!!
R. Chast

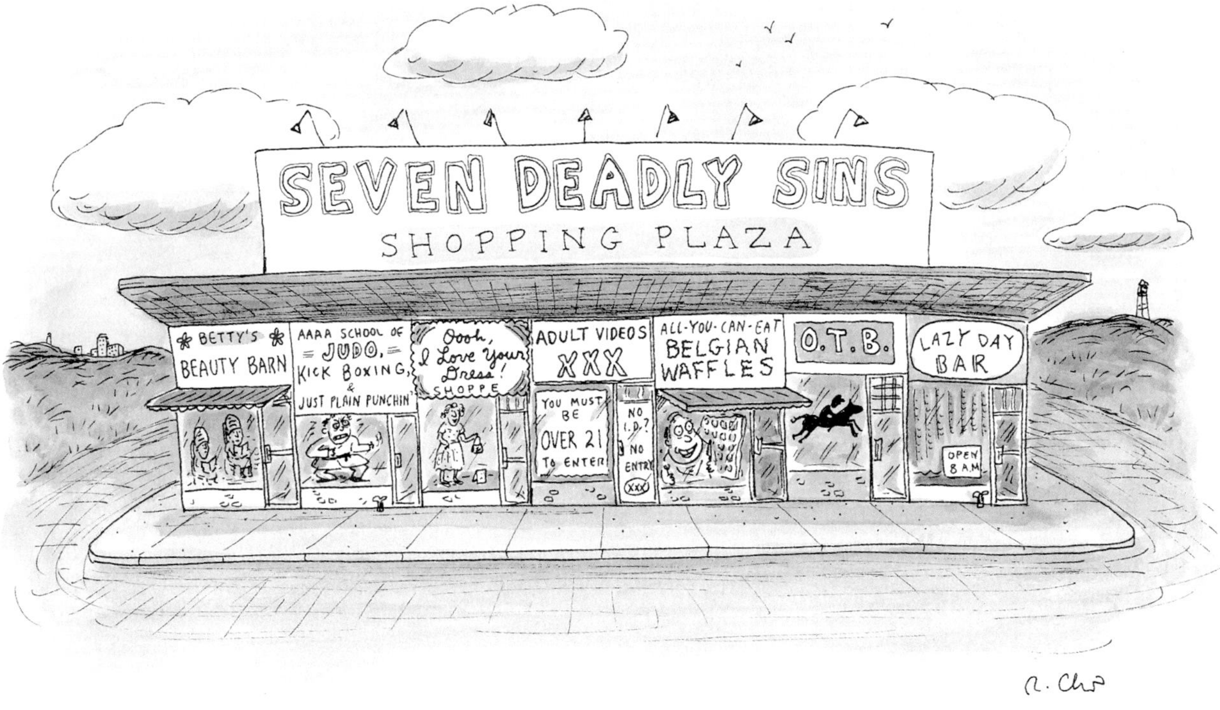
SEVEN DEADLY SINS
SHOPPING PLAZA
BETTY'S
BEAUTY BARN
AAAA SCHOOL OF
JUDO,
KICK BOXING,
&
JUST PLAIN PUNCHIN'
Oooh, I Love Your Dress!
SHOPPE
ADULT VIDEOS
XXX
YOU MUST BE
OVER 21
TO ENTER
NO I.D.?
NO ENTRY
XXX
ALL-YOU-CAN-EAT
BELGIAN
WAFFLES
O.T.B.
LAZY DAY
BAR
OPEN
8 A.M.

FOR THEIR OWN GOOD

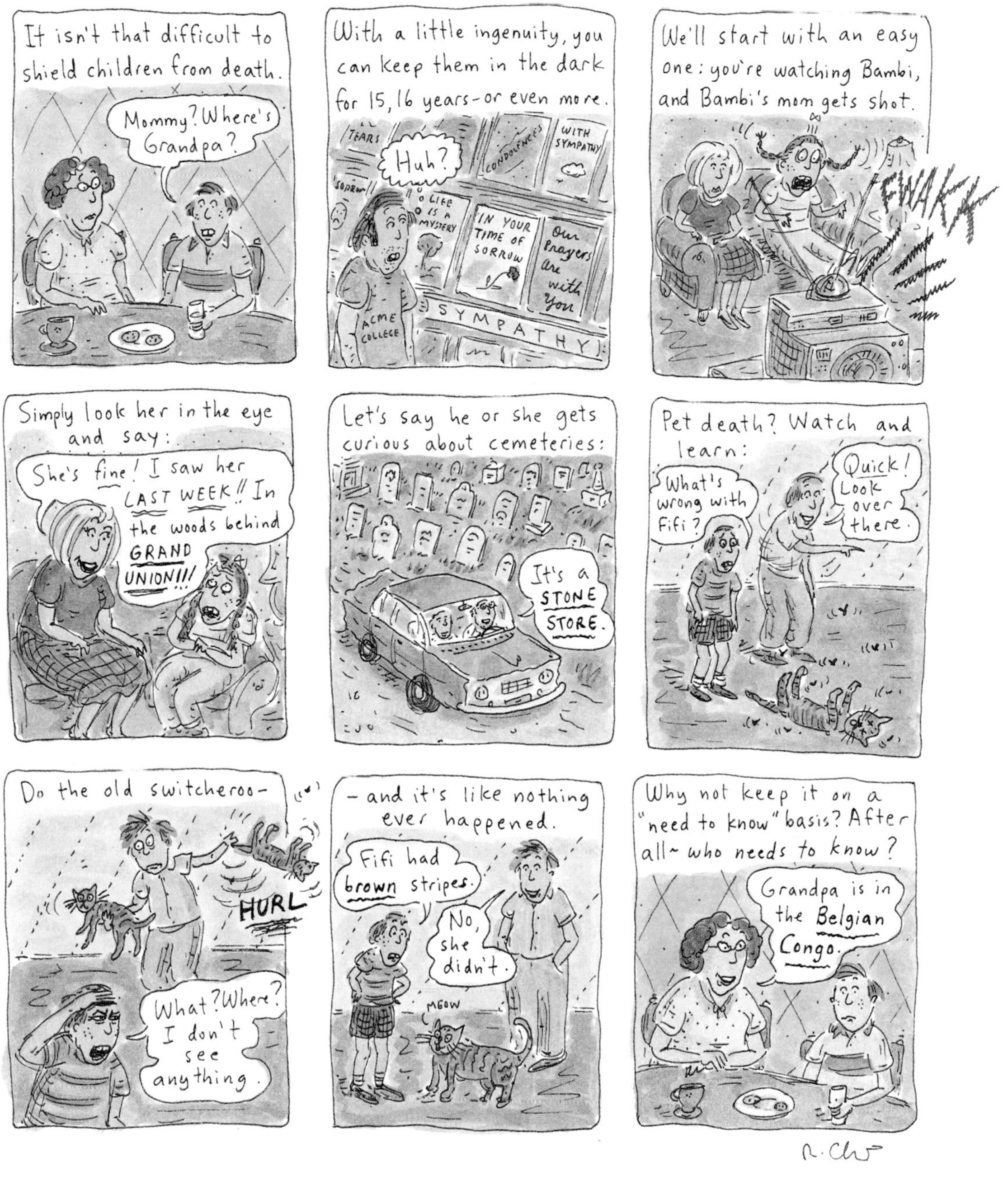
It isn't that difficult to shield children from death.
Mommy? Where's Grandpa?
With a little ingenuity, you can keep them in the dark for 15, 16 years—or even more.
TEARS
SORROW
CONDOLENCES
WITH SYMPATHY
Huh?
LIFE IS A MYSTERY
IN YOUR TIME OF SORROW
Our Prayers Are with You
SYMPATHY
ACME COLLEGE
We'll start with an easy one: you're watching Bambi, and Bambi's mom gets shot.
FWAK
Simply look her in the eye and say:
She's fine! I saw her LAST WEEK!! In the woods behind GRAND UNION!!!
Let's say he or she gets curious about cemeteries:
It's a STONE STORE.
Pet death? Watch and learn:
What's wrong with Fifi?
Quick! Look over there.
Do the old switcheroo—
HURL
What? Where? I don't see anything.
—and it's like nothing ever happened.
Fifi had brown stripes.
No, she didn't.
MEOW
Why not keep it on a "need to know" basis? After all—who needs to know?
Grandpa is in the Belgian Congo.
R. Chast

CHILDREN'S DREAM BEDTIME ROUTINE

7:30 - 8	Brush teeth; wash hands and face.
8 - 8:30	Get school stuff ready for next day.
8:30 - 9	Put pajamas on.
9 - 11	Watch sitcoms.
11 - 11:30	Watch pro wrestling.
11:30 - 12	Say good night to pets.
12 - 12:30	Midnight snack.
12:30 - 1	Video games.
1 - 1:30	Get into bed.
1:30 - 2:30	Reading hour.
2:30 - 3	Water break.
3 - 4	Read-aloud story time.
4 - 4:30	Last-minute fear assuaging.
4:30	Lights out.

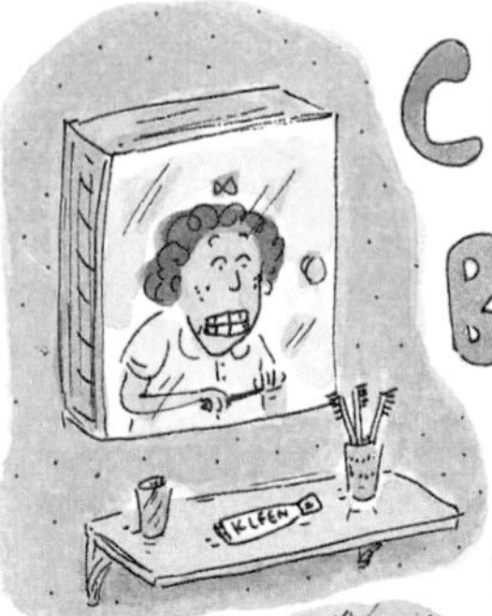

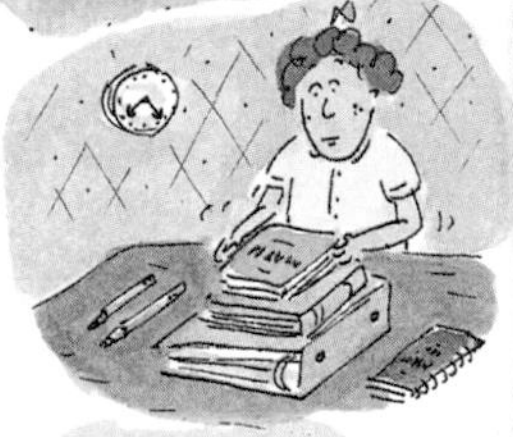

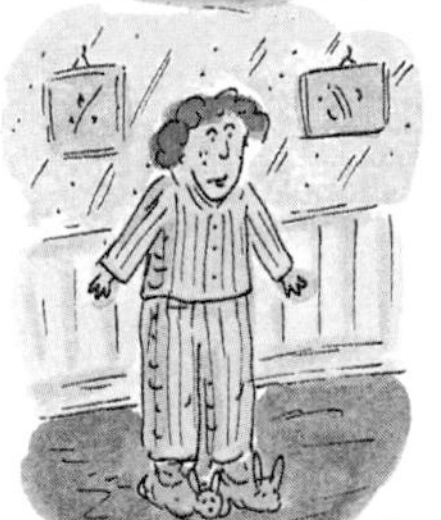

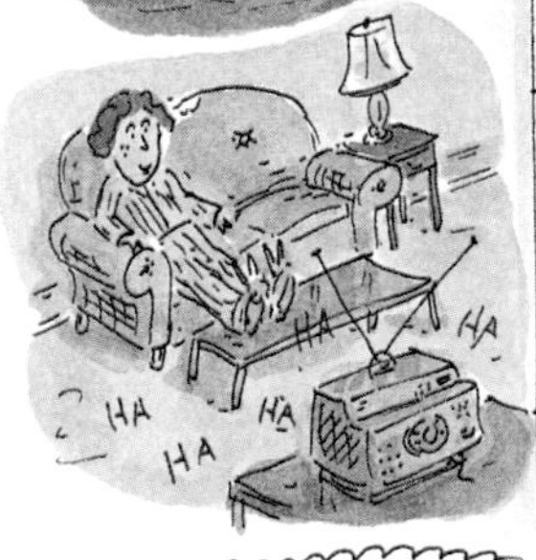
HA
HA
HA
HA
HA

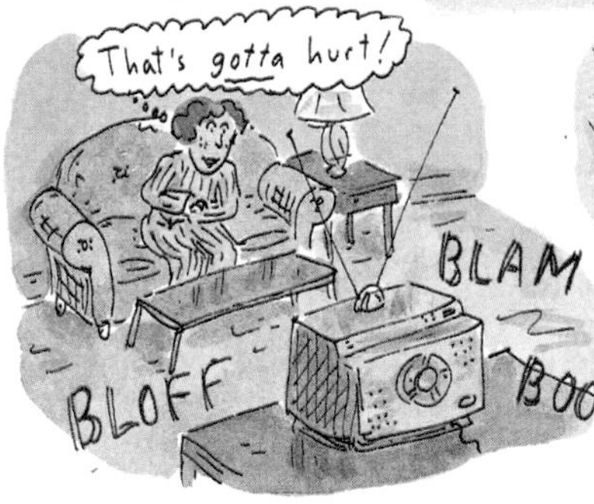
That's gotta hurt!
BLAM
BLOFF
BOOF

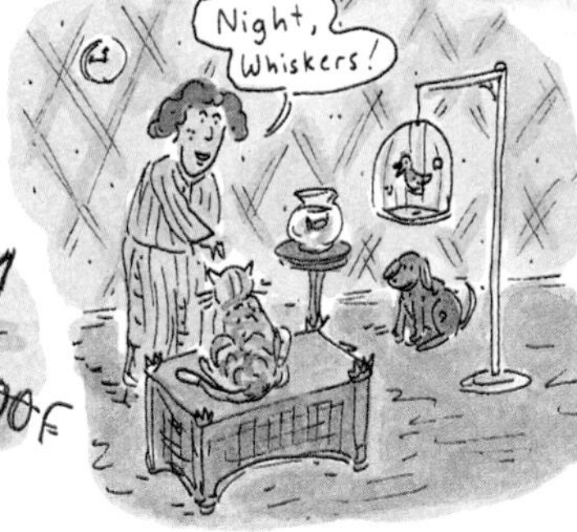
Night, Whiskers!

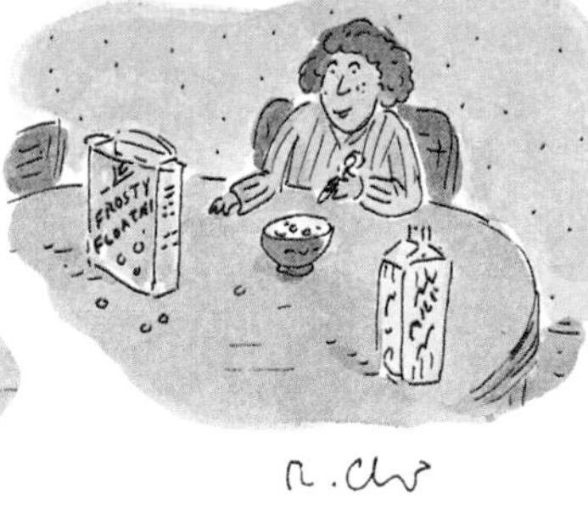
FROSTY FLOATS

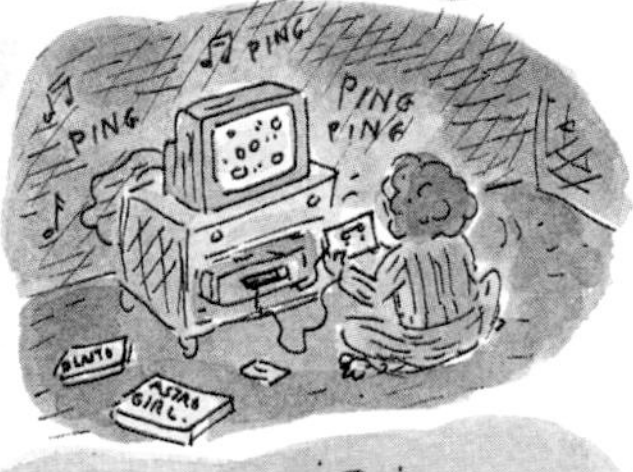
PING
PING
PING
PING

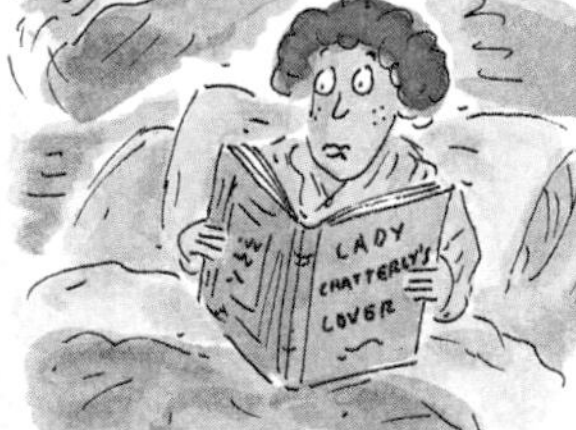
LADY CHATTERLEY'S LOVER

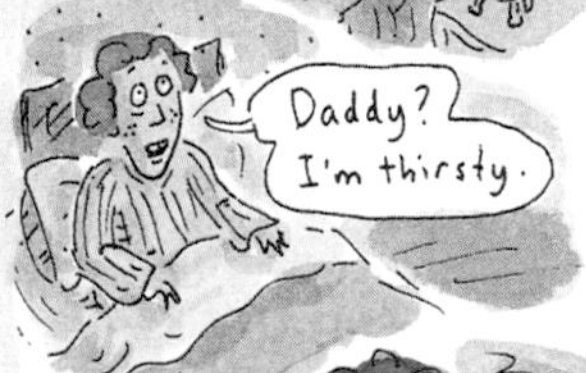
Daddy? I'm thirsty.

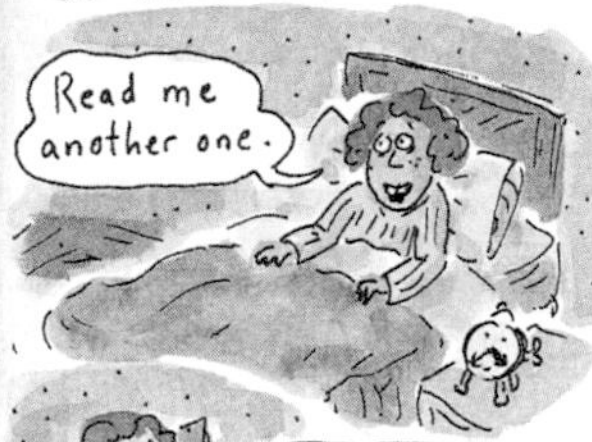
Read me another one.

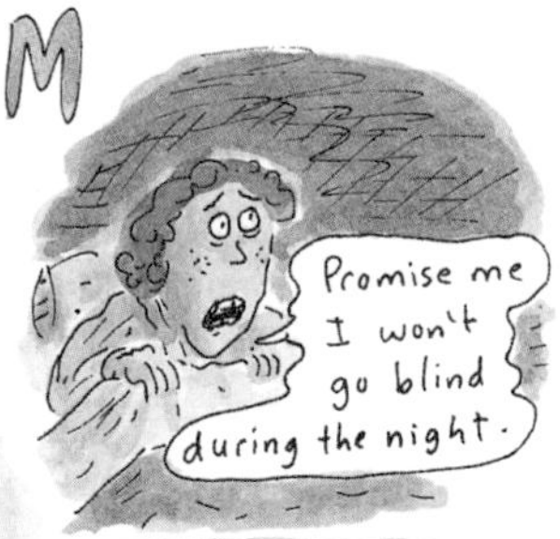
Promise me I won't go blind during the night.

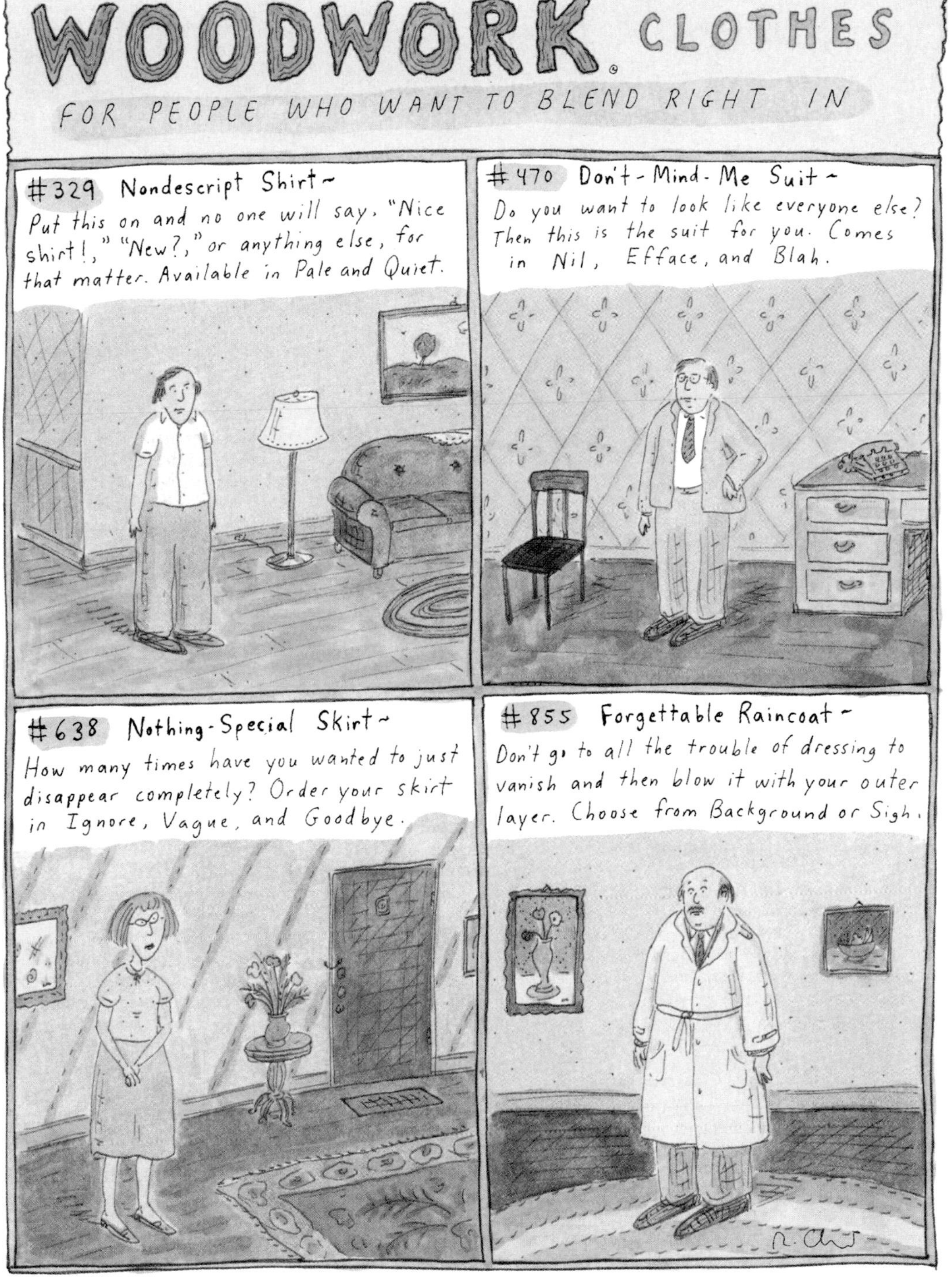
WOODWORK® CLOTHES
FOR PEOPLE WHO WANT TO BLEND RIGHT IN
#329 Nondescript Shirt~
Put this on and no one will say, "Nice shirt!," "New?," or anything else, for that matter. Available in Pale and Quiet.
#470 Don't-Mind-Me Suit~
Do you want to look like everyone else? Then this is the suit for you. Comes in Nil, Efface, and Blah.
#638 Nothing-Special Skirt~
How many times have you wanted to just disappear completely? Order your skirt in Ignore, Vague, and Goodbye.
#855 Forgettable Raincoat~
Don't go to all the trouble of dressing to vanish and then blow it with your outer layer. Choose from Background or Sigh.
R. Chast

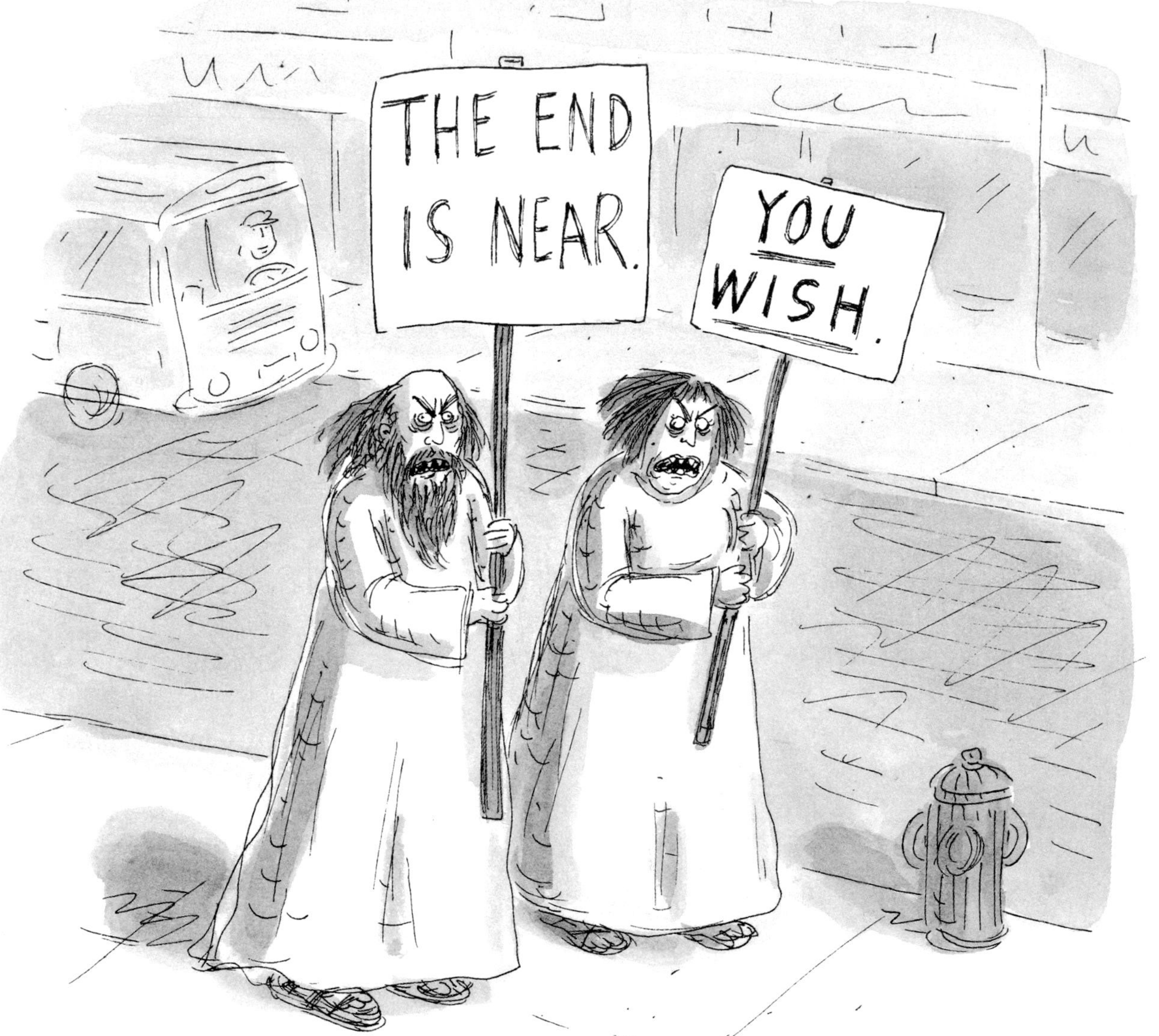
THE END IS NEAR.
YOU WISH.
r. Chst

VIVE LA RÉSISTANCE

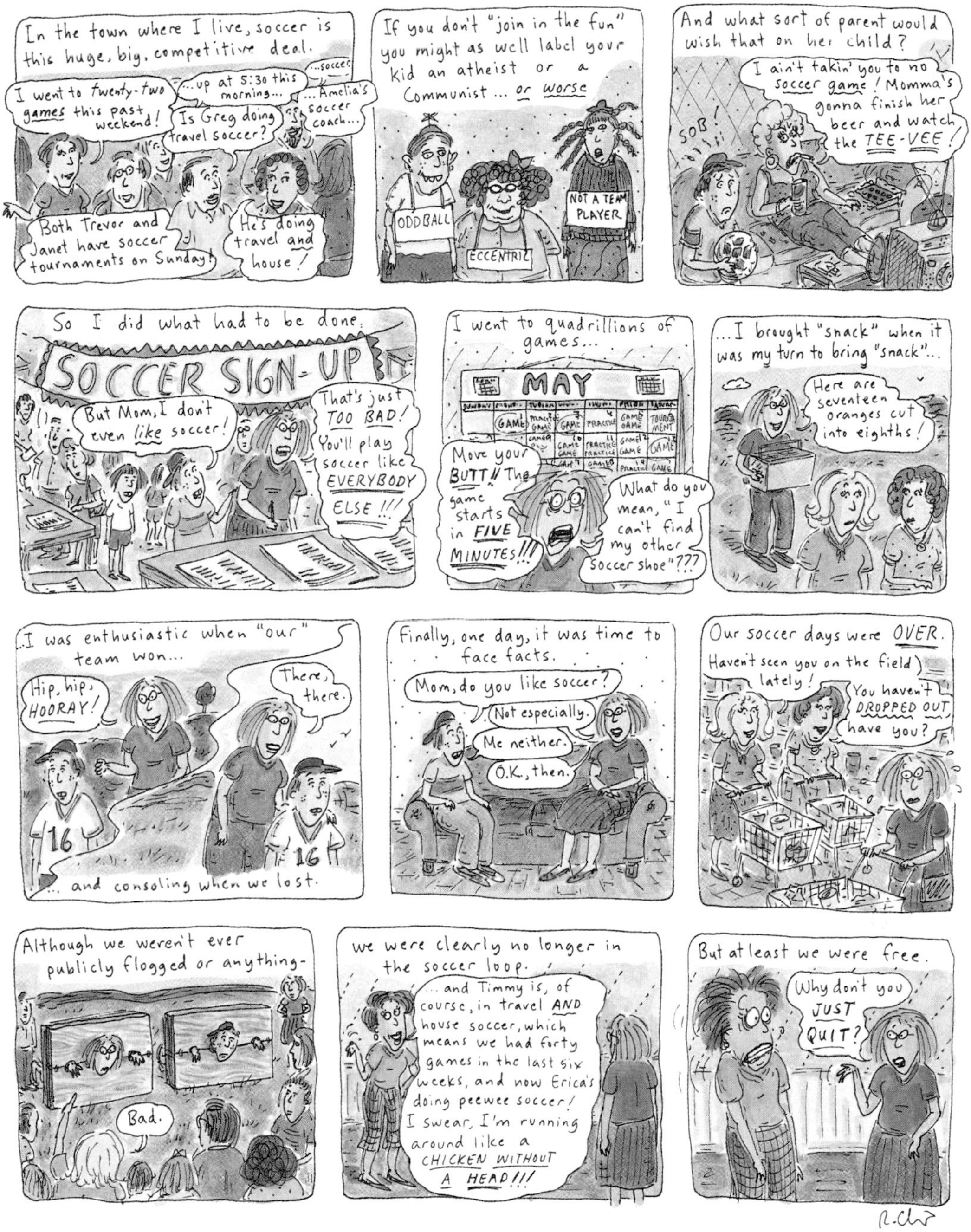
In the town where I live, soccer is this huge, big, competitive deal.
I went to twenty-two games this past weekend!
...up at 5:30 this morning...
...soccer
Is Greg doing travel soccer?
...Amelia's soccer coach...
Both Trevor and Janet have soccer tournaments on Sunday!
He's doing travel and house!
If you don't "join in the fun" you might as well label your kid an atheist or a Communist ... or worse
ODDBALL
ECCENTRIC
NOT A TEAM PLAYER
And what sort of parent would wish that on her child?
I ain't takin' you to no soccer game! Momma's gonna finish her beer and watch the TEE-VEE!
SOB!
So I did what had to be done.
SOCCER SIGN-UP
But Mom, I don't even like soccer!
That's just TOO BAD! You'll play soccer like EVERYBODY ELSE!!!
I went to quadrillions of games...
MAY
Move your BUTT!! The game starts in FIVE MINUTES!!!
What do you mean, "I can't find my other soccer shoe"???
...I brought "snack" when it was my turn to bring "snack"...
Here are seventeen oranges cut into eighths!
...I was enthusiastic when "our" team won...
Hip, hip, HOORAY!
There, there.
16
16
... and consoling when we lost.
Finally, one day, it was time to face facts.
Mom, do you like soccer?
Not especially.
Me neither.
O.K., then.
Our soccer days were OVER.
Haven't seen you on the field lately!
You haven't DROPPED OUT, have you?
Although we weren't ever publicly flogged or anything-
Bad.
we were clearly no longer in the soccer loop.
... and Timmy is, of course, in travel AND house soccer, which means we had forty games in the last six weeks, and now Erica's doing peewee soccer! I swear, I'm running around like a CHICKEN WITHOUT A HEAD!!!
But at least we were free.
Why don't you JUST QUIT?
R. Chast

UNCHARTED WATERS

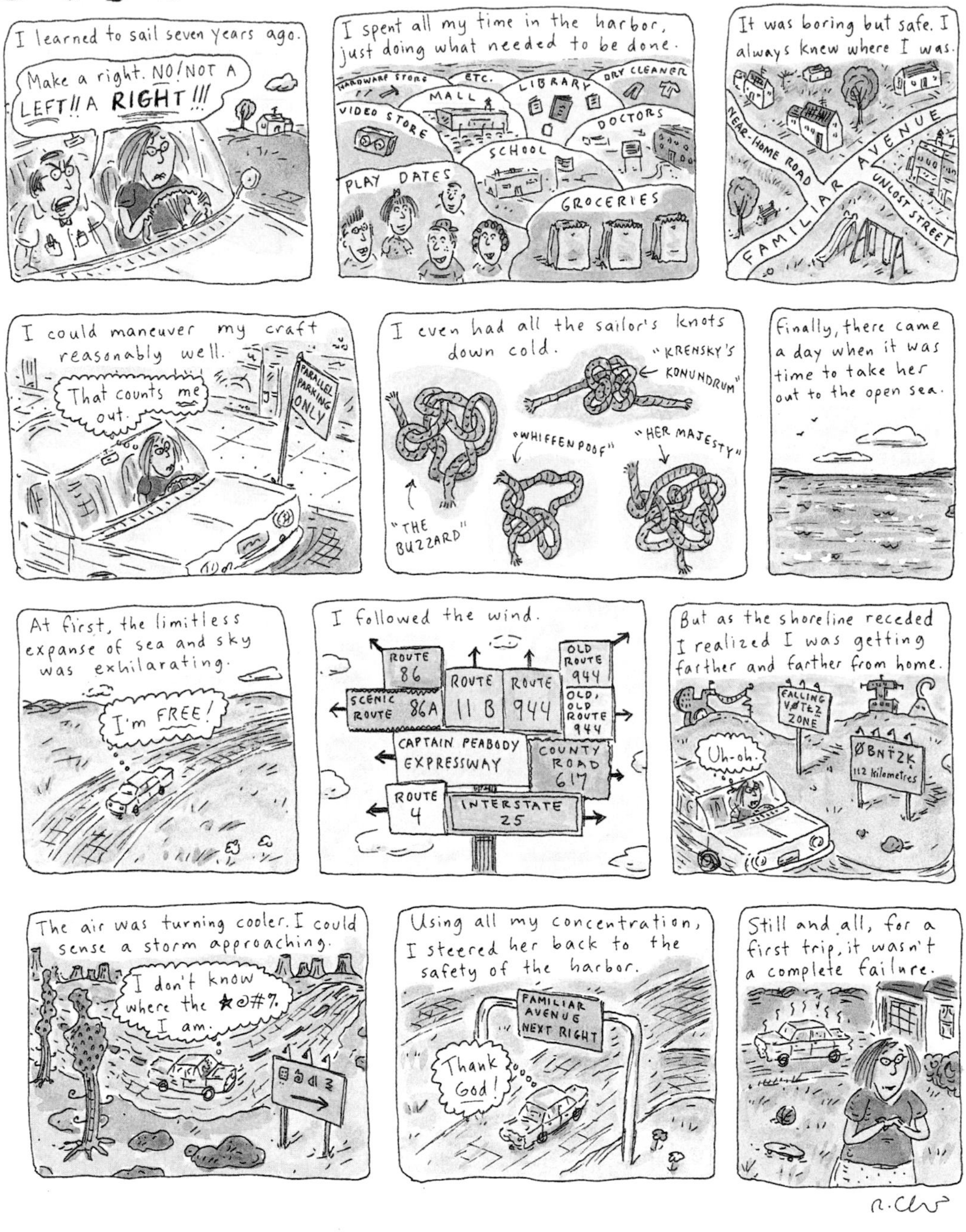

I learned to sail seven years ago.
Make a right. NO! NOT A LEFT!! A RIGHT!!!
I spent all my time in the harbor, just doing what needed to be done.
HARDWARE STORE
ETC.
LIBRARY
DRY CLEANER
MALL
VIDEO STORE
DOCTORS
SCHOOL
PLAY DATES
GROCERIES
It was boring but safe. I always knew where I was.
NEAR-HOME ROAD
AVENUE
FAMILIAR
UNLOST STREET
I could maneuver my craft reasonably well.
That counts me out.
PARALLEL PARKING ONLY
I even had all the sailor's knots down cold.
"KRENSKY'S KONUNDRUM"
"WHIFFENPOOF"
"HER MAJESTY"
"THE BUZZARD"
Finally, there came a day when it was time to take her out to the open sea.
At first, the limitless expanse of sea and sky was exhilarating.
I'm FREE!
I followed the wind.
ROUTE 86
ROUTE 11 B
ROUTE 944
OLD ROUTE 944
SCENIC ROUTE 86A
OLD, OLD ROUTE 944
CAPTAIN PEABODY EXPRESSWAY
COUNTY ROAD 617
ROUTE 4
INTERSTATE 25
But as the shoreline receded I realized I was getting farther and farther from home.
FALLING VØTEZ ZONE
Uh-oh.
ØBNTZK 112 kilometres
The air was turning cooler. I could sense a storm approaching.
I don't know where the ★@#7. I am.
Using all my concentration, I steered her back to the safety of the harbor.
FAMILIAR AVENUE NEXT RIGHT
Thank God!
Still and all, for a first trip, it wasn't a complete failure.
R. Chast

A NOTE ON THE AUTHOR

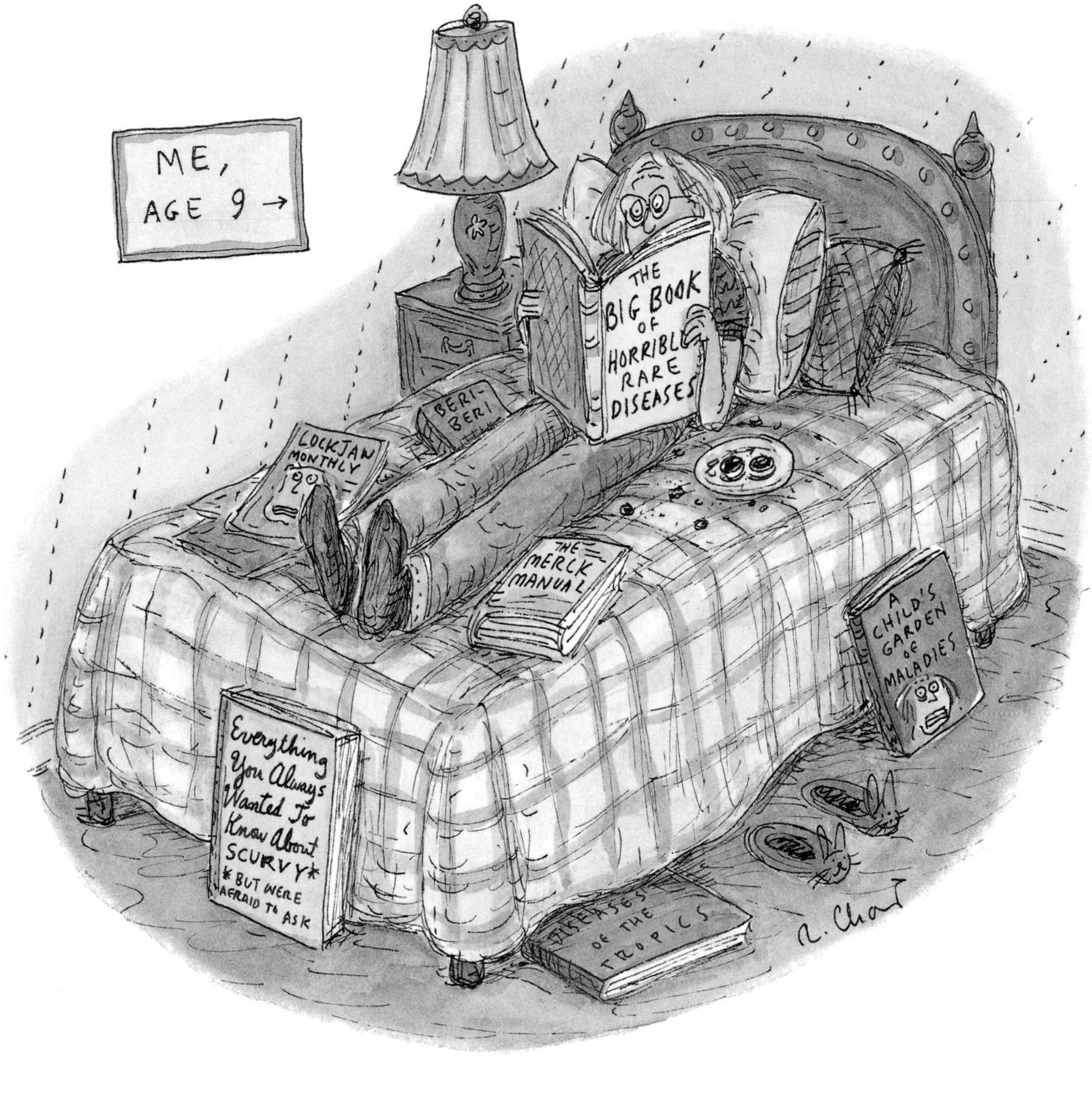
ME,
AGE 9 →
THE BIG BOOK OF HORRIBLE RARE DISEASES
BERI-BERI
LOCKJAW MONTHLY
THE MERCK MANUAL
A CHILD'S GARDEN OF MALADIES
Everything You Always Wanted To Know About SCURVY* *BUT WERE AFRAID TO ASK
DISEASES OF THE TROPICS
R. Chast

A NOTE ON THE TYPE

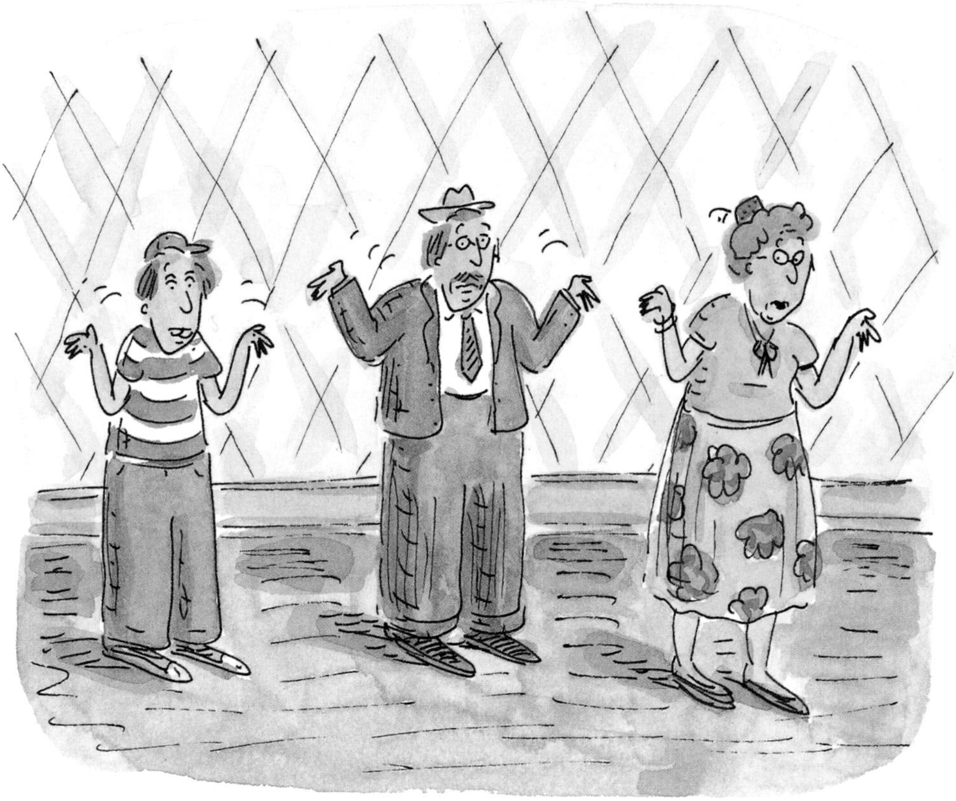